D0090283

Catholic
Does Not Equal
The Vatican

Catholic
Does Not Equal
the Vatican

A VISION FOR

PROGRESSIVE CATHOLICISM

Rosemary Radford Ruether

THE NEW PRESS

NEW YORK
LONDON

Requests for permission to reproduce selections from this book should be
mailed to: Permissions Department, The New Press, 38 Greene Street,
New York, NY 10013.

Published in the United States by The New Press, New York, 2008
Distributed by W. W. Norton & Company, Inc., New York

LIBRARY OF CONGRESS CATALOGING-IN-PUBLICATION DATA

Ruether, Rosemary Radford.
Catholic does not equal the Vatican : a vision for progressive Catholicism /
Rosemary Radford Ruether.
p.   cm.
Includes bibliographical references.
ISBN 978-1-59558-406-9 (hc.)
1. Liberalism (Religion)—Catholic Church.   2. Catholic Church—
History—21st century.   I. Title.
BX1396.2.R84   2008
282.09'0511—dc22   2008008735

The New Press was established in 1990 as a not-for-profit alternative to
the large, commercial publishing houses currently dominating the book
publishing industry. The New Press operates in the public interest rather
than for private gain, and is committed to publishing, in innovative ways,
works of educational, cultural, and community value that are often deemed
insufficiently profitable.

www.thenewpress.com

Composition by dix!
This book was set in New Caledonia

Printed in the United States of America

2   4   6   8   10   9   7   5   3   1

Contents

Foreword
Susan Brooks Thistlethwaite

I was so happy to get my hands on the manuscript of this new book by Rosemary Ruether. I count on Rosemary for a blast furnace of feminist theology, and she has yet to disappoint me. When I open her books, a roar comes out, a force of mind and heart that simply *will not* submit to patriarchy. This book is that power turned to the task of making right what has been rendered so wrong for so long. *Catholic Does Not Equal the Vatican* is vintage Ruether, as bracing as her earliest works and just as powerful.

I became a feminist theologian the day Rosemary Radford Ruether gave a lecture at my seminary, Duke Divinity School. This is absolutely true. There were only five women in my class at Duke when I entered. I went to seminary out of antiwar work, not out of any strong feminist consciousness (though I had gone to Smith College, so I think there was a little unconscious feminism lurking even then). I saw a poster that advertised a guest lecturer with a woman's name—unusual in the early 1970s. And then I looked at the title. She was going to talk about "women's anger." I still remember the frisson of fear and enjoyment that the juxtaposition of the words "women" and "anger" evoked in me as I looked at that poster on the seminary wall. I decided to attend.

The lecture hall was auditorium-style and the all-male faculty chose to sit together at the back, at the top, in the last row. Even today I can hardly think of that choice of location without chuckling at their vivid demonstration of the exact problem that Ruether was about to address. Three women students, myself included, sat in the front row. And all the male students sat in between. Rosemary entered, smiling and friendly, and she immediately dropped her papers. As she gathered them up from the desk and the floor, she joked about "getting my anger together" and then calmly went on to shatter every vestige of my theological beliefs. I came in a woman seminary student and left a feminist theologian. It is as simple as that. And it is a story repeated over and over for an entire generation of feminist theologians Rosemary inspired.

The fundamental point Ruether makes over and over throughout the whole corpus of her many works is the nature of dualism, the radically oppositionalist thinking that funds the "isms" that break apart human community across the centuries and across cultures. Sexism is the original dualism. With her long and deep historical view, Ruether has documented the hierarchy of men over women, which creates civilization with its rigid and abiding edifices of power and control. Dualism creates dualism: men over women, reason over nature, transcendence over immanence, rich over poor, white over black, Christian over Jew, and on and on and on. These dualisms double back on themselves, the oppressed and the oppressors even taking turns, but the model remains the same. We versus they.

Ruether is a true liberation theologian. She grounds her theological work in the history of culture and then applies the searing scope of the gospel to what she sees. This new work is no exception: "The perennial meaning of the gospel is rooted in the person and ministry of Jesus Christ." We need Jesus the liberator, Christ the source of grace for the power to confront domination and proclaim the year of the Lord's favor.

Hers is a timely message. We face not only a Catholic Church wrapped in its own power and privilege, increasingly blind to the real church in its midst of women, the poor, the many nations represented among the faithful and their rich differences, but also a political system that is the mirror image of what Ruether says about the Catholic Church. As I was reading her section on "infallibility" in relationship to the Catholic Church hierarchy, I thought how her criticism fits the Bush administration as well. The illusion that one cannot be mistaken is a demonic blunder, precluding repentance and change. It is death by idolatry—truly, it is.

The world needs a different message from the official Catholic Church in the twenty-first century than it is getting. The abuse of nature is catching up with us in the violent and destructive effects of global warming; Cold War rhetoric about nuclear weapons is heating up again and nuclear proliferation is again a threat; the demonization of other religions is on the rise. Instead of a prophetic stance against these evils (and many others!) the Catholic Church is overly preoccupied with dualistic views of human sexuality and reviving the Latin Mass. It is time for someone to say "basta!" Enough! That person is Rosemary Ruether.

In a truly just world, Rosemary Radford Ruether would be Pope. Until then, this book is a great "encyclical" about the grace of God and the liberating work to which the true church is called.

Amen and amen.

Introduction

The Roman Catholic Church worldwide is deeply polarized, divided between progressive and reactionary directions. During the pontificate of Pope John Paul II there was a systematic effort to undo the openness to ecumenism, modern scholarship, and social justice begun with the Second Vatican Council in the 1960s. In 2007 it seems unlikely that institutional Catholicism, as defined by the Vatican, can move in any direction except backward, not back to the Gospels, but back to Vatican I, back to a defensive posture of a papal monarchy, claiming infallibility and seeking to impose its will upon the global church and upon the world outside the Catholic Church. It has placed reactionary Opus Dei members in episcopal positions in country after country. It has appointed them to delegations to the United Nations and the European Union in a bid for control in world affairs. The Vatican has not only placed reactionary Catholic leaders in places of influence around the world, it has also sought to dismantle the institutions and programs that progressive Catholics have developed to promote a liberative vision of justice.

This book is the story of progressive Catholics and Catholic movements in the world that refuse to move backward with the Vatican, that refuse to surrender our church to fearful, reactionary leaders in its ecclesial hierarchies. Our Catholicism is not merely one option within world Catholicism; it is, in our view, a more authentic Catholicism, shorn of its imperial biases and alliances with Eurocentric ruling classes. The Roman Catholic Church has reached a crucial moment in its history, and there is no more important time for progressive Catholics to stay committed to an alternative vision of Catholic Christianity.

There are many Catholics and former Catholics who see any effort to stay committed to church reform as increasingly futile, perhaps even masochistic—certainly a waste of energy better spent doing other more productive things. We need to look the negative character of the reactionary drive of the hierarchical church government full in the face and not minimize its seriousness, but also without confusing it with the ultimate ground of our faith, hope, and love for the church. We should not equate Vatican policies with essential Roman Catholicism. Our foundations lie in Jesus Christ and a vision of the church as a new humanity freed from all forms of violence and oppression. It is our firm rooting in this ultimate ground that we most need if we are to stay the course as prophetic reformers in the Catholic Church at this time.

My vision of the church is shaped by an effort to respond to the Kairos of this period of human history, a time when the hopes released by the end of the Cold War have been betrayed by a new American imperialist militarism, a time when we must stand in horror at the increasing gaps between wealth and poverty in the world as a whole, and at the accelerating devastation of the earth caused by profligate and unjust materialism. We ourselves are often torn both by our sense of urgency and our feelings of helplessness before these challenges. Yet my vision of the church is also shaped by what I believe is the perennial meaning of the gospel, rooted in the person and ministry of Jesus Christ, ever new and yet ever one in a wisdom beyond the vicissitudes of historical developments.

To me that transcendent wisdom—and I do consciously use the word "transcendent" in what I see as its authentic sense—is summed up by the word "grace," a grace that is the authentic being of God made present to us in the life, death, and resurrection of Christ, that both liberates us from the deformations of our power and security grabbing, and returns us to our deeper and authentic self and calling as God's good creation. To me, being the church, the body of Christ, is basically about being the community who lives in and through that life of grace.

For me, Roman Catholicism is not the "only true church" or even the best church, but it is a very important expression of historical Christianity in the West, and its reform and renewal are vital to the many around the world who are part of this church, as well as to many others who are affected by its presence and power. The progressive Catholicism that many of us have helped create in the last half century must be defended. We represent an ecumenical Catholic Christianity; we acknowledge the truth of other Christian churches, as well as world religions, while at the same time remaining committed to our own particular tradition. Though there are vehement forces within Catholicism that wish to contest and even drive out this progressive Catholicism, we must keep it alive and maintain its vision.

THE CHURCH WE NEED NOW

In discussing the church we need now, the church we have always needed, the church we were called to be from the beginning and are called to be today, both as local churches and as global church, I will explore the following six elements of an authentic Catholicism in depth.

1. *It Is Multicultural*

We are called to be authentically "catholic," that is universal, not hegemonic white male Euroamericans who confuse white male Western culture with normative human and Christian culture, to be imposed on other peoples, on indigenous people, on Africans, Asians, Arabs, and Polynesians. This means really exploring, claiming, and celebrating the actual cultural diversity of our Catholic people around the world. This also means paying particular attention to the peoples who are the descendents of brutal colonization and enslavements imposed by European conquests over the centuries: the indigenous peoples of the Americas and the Pacific, and the African peoples brought to the Americas in chains.

Globally Catholics are increasingly Hispanic, African, and Asian, even as the old heartlands of European Catholicism in Italy, France, Ireland, and Spain have grown apathetic and their offspring in North America have followed suit. Since 1965, immigration has also infused Catholic life in the United States with people from Asia, the Middle East, Latin America, the Caribbean, and Africa. Yet we are still a people wedded to cultural patterns shaped in the European Middle Ages and a church polity formed by fourth-century Roman imperialism and eighteenth-century absolute monarchy, seeking to live on as ecclesiastical verities after the political foundations have died. We need to acknowledge the relativity and even the demonic character of these hegemonic cultural and political forms of the past. At the same time, we need to embrace a rich dialogue between the many cultures that make up the Catholic people, for the transformation and mutual enrichment of our whole cultural and social life.

2. *It Acknowledges Its Fallibility*

A church that believes itself infallible in the pronouncements of its monarchical ruler is a church that has encapsulated itself in its own apostasy and made that apostasy irredeemable. The mistaken claim of papal infallibility was imposed at a particularly bad moment in late-nineteenth-century Italian Catholic history. In my view as a theologian, every other sin is forgivable except this sin of claiming to be infallible, because it is a sin against the Holy Spirit. This does not mean we cannot repent of it. But we cannot repent of this or any mistake we have ever made, or are making, unless we acknowledge that we indeed can err, not simply as individuals, but as an institution acting in its formal and public capacity.

The error of infallibility fixates all other errors, and to repent of it is also to liberate ourselves to be human, knowing ourselves to be finite, fallible, and able to see only in part, not absolutely or with final certainty. Knowing our fallibility liberates us to be Christian, to live by faith, repentance, and the grace of transformation, gifts of the Spirit without which we cannot be in authentic continuity with the new life in Christ and in authentic relationship with each other. For new life in Christ can only be born and continually reborn through death to our idolatries and resurrection to a life that we hold not by grasping it, but only by being upheld by the one in whom alone we have ultimate trust. This ultimate trust excludes not only formulaic certainties of doctrines and teaching authorities, whether of Pope or Bible, but also liberates us from an infantile need for such certainties, from a desperate clinging to a demand for absolute truth. It liberates us to search intelligently for the perspectival truths that we can construct, but that we know are always fallible and embedded in our cultural contexts and social locations.

We need to analyze clearly and critique in detail the church's many mistakes and the tragic consequences of its claims of infallibility. For example, we must call on the Vatican to repent of its teachings about birth control, about the exclusion of all women and married and gay men from ordination, about the spiritual superiority of celibacy, and about the divine sanction for patriarchal hierarchy. The Vatican must repent specifically, not just vaguely and in abstract terms that leave confusion or doubt about what it said. But none of these reforms is possible without first admitting the possibility of error.

3. *It Lives by Grace*

The church we seek, in which alone we can have life, is a church that lives by a grace. This grace does not exclude knowledge, experience, and historical change; rather, it is a grace that upholds us and supports us in and through our searches for meaning and justice. Through grace we receive freedom to repent, liberating us from misplaced ideas and systems and renewing us in the miracle of life that wells up fresh every day.

4. *It Is Liberated from Sexism*

It is particularly at this time that we need to deepen our commitment to a Christian community that is a community of equals, a community in which the distinctions of male and female have been overcome in the new humanity, where both women and men are recognized as images of God and representatives of Christ. We must affirm women as preachers, as sacramental ministers, and as theologians, and we must bring women's gifts of ministry fully into the church for the first time. We also need to affirm that being in Christ restores us to the fullness of life in all dimensions of the flesh, as well as of the spirit. This fullness includes female bodies and every body's capacity to give love and pleasure to another, without fear, and also without irresponsibility or exploitation.

To contemplate a church liberated from sexism requires us to be deeply repentant and transformed from much of what has been our history. Yet today, sexism and its twin, sexual pathology, seem more rampant in church leaders than ever. The Vatican rejects the ordination of women and forbids contraception as if these were the first articles of faith. The Vatican clings to a misguided concept of unchanging truth when it insists on a celibate male priesthood and opposes any possibility of married priests, women priests, or openly gay priests, while actual celibate male priests are increasingly few and some find themselves discredited by charges of sexual abuse of children.

The previous Pope sanctified two Italian women victims as saints and role models for women. One, who was pregnant, died of uterine cancer rather than save her own life; she left a newborn baby and four other motherless children. The other endured continual spousal abuse rather than leave her husband, who abandoned her. We must reject these kinds of models and roles for women. Progressive Catholics must renew the ways Christians live as community with one another. We must commit to living equally and mutually as women and men who are liberated from sexual pathology into healthy, loving forms of sexuality and who affirm a diversity of sexual orientations and identities.

5. *It Is Democratic*

For forty years or more Catholics have been creating "base communities," in which small groups of ten to fifteen people covenant together for regular prayer, study, worship, discussion, and mutual support. Whether or not we have reasonable parish communities where we feel nourished in weekly worship, these base communities are an important support for Christian life. Such base communities were an integral part of the church created by Latin American liberation theology in the last three decades. But in many cases, these base communities remained too clerical and too dependent on bishops; they failed to address adequately many of the pressing issues of daily life, particularly issues of women and of sexual and domestic abuse. We need to recommit ourselves to developing these communities in a way that will be deeper, more long-lasting, and more liberating for all members.

The historic church patterned itself after patriarchy, aristocracy, and monarchy, making itself an obstacle to modern democratic movements and the democratization of the church. When bishops thunder that the "church is not a democracy," they do not intend to speak merely about historical and social facts, but about divine intention. In their minds, Christ founded the church to be a centralized feudal monarchy: Pope over bishops, bishops over priests, priests over laity, men over women, and all adults over children. They believe that this church structure is what Christ intended.

That this whole pattern of hierarchy might have been historically accidental, modeled on existing political systems, and, even worse, a betrayal of a deeper vision of the church as a community of equals, better expressed in patterns of community where all members have a voice and a share in ministry, is unthinkable to such bishops. But it is precisely the historically accidental and non-normative nature of such hierarchical structures that must be understood today. For anyone with a minimal acquaintance with the New Testament and church history, the historical and accidental character of such hierarchical structures is obvious.

6. *It Is Committed to the Poor and the Oppressed*

Since the post–World War II birth of liberation theologies in Latin America, Africa, and Asia, our brothers and sisters from these regions have been calling the church to renew itself through a preferential option for the poor. The Christian church is authentically the body of Christ only when it lives in solidarity with those who are treated unjustly, those who are the most marginalized and despised, and those who are made destitute by systems of power and wealth. The foundational call of Christ to repentance, ministry, and service was and remains "good news to the poor, the liberation of the captive, the setting at liberty of those who are oppressed." When we live that good news, we live the gospel.

To live that good news after twenty centuries of Catholic history is also to live by repentance, to live in deep mourning and contrition in the struggle to change what has overwhelmingly been and still is a contrary reality. To live good news to the poor is to resist ecclesiastical power and privilege rooted in a preferential option for the rich and powerful. Since at least the early fourth century, Catholic Christianity has grown in wealth and power. It blessed the power of aristocracies, of emperors and kings, of merchants, and of capitalist corporations, and their economic, political, and military might. Church leaders have mostly advised the poor and the oppressed to win favor with God by obeying their masters. If Christ calls us to be faithful by our solidarity with the poor, then Christ calls Catholics to be a counter-sign to most of what the church has been during its history.

HOW DO WE GET THERE FROM HERE?

Once we have sketched something of our vision of authentic Christian community, the key question is how do we get there from here? What are the ways of moving toward that vision, given the present church polity and ideology which mostly institutionalizes and sanctifies its opposite? There are five ways we can begin to change ourselves and to build organizational bases to support such alternatives.

First, we need to *grow up.* Traditional Catholic socialization breeds a spirituality of infantilism. We have great difficulty really liberating ourselves from the residue of a spirituality of childlike dependence that has been deeply bred into our psyches.

Catholicism, like all patriarchal hierarchical institutions, recreates relationships of domination and submission, modeled on relations of male over female and parent over child. We learn to dominate those below us and submit to those above us, but we do not learn how to be equals in mutually affirming relationships. We are not encouraged to become genuinely autonomous adults, but rather to remain always a dependent child under some kind of higher authority. These patterns of relationship are central to clerical culture, in which priests are literally called "Father," even by those older than they are.

This socialization into paternalistic dependency fixates Catholics between rebellion and submission. We often revert back to submission to assuage feelings of guilt for rebellion and are not freed to be genuinely responsible adults. By responsible adults, I mean people who have confidence in their own mind and agency, without self-inflation or self-negation. An adult is able to take responsibility for helping to develop the future of a community without needing either to assuage guilt or to assert her or his power through such service. This maturity is required for real ministry, but it is difficult to develop in a paternalistic system.

Second, we need to be people of *prayer.* This means we have to overcome the split between spirituality and social action that has been endemic in our culture and squeezes the presence of God out of real life. Our ability to stay the course of social and church change for the long haul is only possible when we have a deep grounding in the disciplines of daily prayer and meditation and we cultivate divine presence in our lives. Finding time for quiet meditation on a regular basis allows us to resist workaholism and the society's demands for endless achievement. The discipline of prayer cultivates a sense of the presence of God, even in the midst of intense activity.

Disciplines of prayer have been part of traditional spirituality, but they were often done under compulsion and with an alienating spirituality that split spirit and body. As we cast off these alienating power relations and views of ourselves, we must not let the practice of prayer fall away. Instead, we must discover how to reclaim it and to create modes of prayer that are really nurturing and nourishing of our whole, adult selves.

Third, we must acquire *critical knowledge* about church history and theology. This knowledge gives us the tools of historical study and theological reflection. These tools enable us to discern what Christian themes are really meaningful and what truth claims need to be questioned as assertions of power that damage our spiritual health. Many of us are already theologically trained people who have been in ministry, so it may seem beside the point to say that we need to be better educated in theology and church history. However, one of the things I learned thirty years ago from a dialogue between the Women's Ordination Conference and the Catholic bishops' Committee on Women was that the seminary education of priests is woefully inadequate.

The bishops who were part of this Committee lacked critical education in the Bible or church history, so they were unable to sort out the questions being put by feminist theologians. The bishops could only follow the assertions of the Vatican that topics like women's ordination were against church

tradition and could not be discussed. In fact, they tended to
say, simply, that women's ordination could not be discussed
because church authority had said so. They could not even
conceive of any independent investigation of this claim from
Scripture and church history.

Fourth, we need to be *socially and ecologically committed.* A preferential option for the poor and an ecological
lifestyle cannot just be rhetorical slogans. They have to relate
to the way we live our lives. Like taking time for prayer, this
commitment calls for rearrangement in our lives. It will impact how some of us make a living. It will require most of us
to examine our wealth and the ways we use energy and resources. It will ask all of us to be in solidarity with those less
fortunate and to live more sustainably with the earth. We
must be part of organized efforts to create an alternative society against the present global (dis)order being imposed by
the World Trade Organization and the powerful nations. We
need a global uprising against the triumphalism of the rich
and powerful who wish to make it appear as if there is no
other alternative possible to the neoliberalism that is impoverishing the earth and the majority of people on the earth.

We need to take ecological impoverishment as seriously
as the poverty of humans. We should recognize that these are
not separate topics but part of one and the same picture. We
must bring the ecological question home to our daily lives
and examine how the way we live everyday is part of the
problem of global impoverishment of the earth and all its in-
habitants. Obviously, ecological sustainability cannot be ac-
complished solely by changes in private lifestyles. We are

part of a vast macrosystem of production, consumption, and waste. But we need to cultivate a certain awareness of how we participate in this system and make adjustments in how we transport ourselves, consume food and goods, use energy, and discard wastes. We need especially to build these shifts into our households, schools, offices, and other local institutions over which have some influence. From this base in consciousness and concrete struggles for ecological sustainability, we may then be able to build larger networks to change the patterns of earth destruction that are diminishing the life of regions and the globe at a macrolevel.

Fifth, we need to build *alternative church communities and organizations.* As I mentioned before, there is already a long history in Catholicism of creating base communities or small worshipping and support groups for liturgy and mutual support. These developments need to continue and become much more common as a resource for Catholics. In addition to small covenant groups, parallel organizations are important to support church reform and social action. American culture, with its tradition of volunteerism, is already rich in creating parallel Catholic organizations. These extend the boundaries of Catholic activity in ways that are not dependent on hierarchical approval. Call to Action; Peace and Justice Centers, such as the Quixote Center in Washington, DC; the Association of the Rights of Catholics in the Church; the Women-Church Convergence; CORPUS, an association of married Catholic priests; Catholics for a Free Choice; and Pax Christi are parallel organizations that are increasingly carving out new frontiers of Catholic life and action.

Why call such groups Catholic? For the simple reason that they see themselves as Catholic, both because their membership is based on people with Catholic roots and because they see themselves as addressing reform issues in the Catholic Church, and doing the work of ministry inspired by Catholic Christian faith and life. In short, these groups see themselves as being church. Their Catholic identity is self-chosen out of a sense of taking responsibility for being the church and calling the institutional church to open itself to this vital work. Yet they are also free of the sort of institutional control that would close them down or dismiss their leaders.

What follows in this book are snapshots of progressive Catholicism that provide a vision for the future. Chapter 1 details something of my own biography and development as a progressive Catholic. Chapter 2 tackles the most morally contradictory aspect of the Vatican's relationship to the majority of Roman Catholics: its position on reproductive rights and women's moral agency. In chapter 3, I describe the key elements of the church's mission in the world for progressive Catholics. Chapter 4 expands the vision of the women-church movement. This movement reflects a core commitment to feminism that is a strand through all my work. In chapter 5, I describe the understanding of church as a discipleship of equals. In chapter 6, I discuss the important work of liberation and ecofeminist theologies in Latin America that have been in the vanguard of shaping a liberative Catholicism. Finally, to show the specious reasoning that defines the Vatican's untenable relationship to women in the church, I present a satiric essay reversing the traditional arguments against women's ordination to argue why men should not be ordained.

Ultimately, progressive Catholics are engaged in a process the future of which cannot be predicted. It may be that those of us concerned with such reforms will grow tired of institutional intransigence and go elsewhere, or it may be that at least parts of the official institution will open itself to greater acceptance of such movements. I hope that we are engaged in a process that will lead to eventual transformation of the official institution to allow legitimacy to the broader range of thought and life. But meanwhile, we can and must carry on living ways of being a Christian community that satisfy our vision of what is authentic and truthful. In short, we need to insist on being the church today and not waiting to be allowed to do so in some distant future.

1

On Being a Progressive Catholic

I grew up in a family that was simultaneously Roman Catholic, ecumenical, and interfaith. I have both maintained and expanded these roots throughout my life as a scholar, a Catholic activist, and an author of over forty books and many hundreds of articles. My mother was a Roman Catholic of English and Austro-Hungarian extraction who was born in Mexico in 1895 and grew up there and in Southern California. She took her religion seriously with regular prayer, daily Mass, and serious reading. However, she had little patience with what she saw as "vulgar Catholicism," superstition, or clerical authoritarianism. She passed on to her daughters a sense that the tradition should both be taken seriously and thought about freely and critically. She regarded nuns and priests who made people feel guilty about asking questions as backward and uneducated.

My father was an Episcopalian whose religion was more a social and class identity than a personal experience. His family belonged to Trinity Episcopal Church in Washington, DC, for generations, and I sometimes accompanied him on the few occasions he went to church at Christmas and Easter. My favorite uncle, David Sandow, my father's brother-in-law, was a Jew whose religion was also more a culture than a personal practice. He was a musician and painter and acted as a surrogate father to my sisters and me when our father was in France during World War II. He imbued us with a lifelong love of the arts. I grew up assuming that these other faiths were to be respected, but in terms of seriousness of personal commitment there was not much contest with my mother's Catholic faith.

After my father's death in 1948 we moved to Southern California, my mother's family home. Several of her socially engaged women friends attended the local Friends' meeting, because they appreciated its pacifist views. I went with them from time to time, in addition to attending Mass with my mother. I learned early in life that I could immerse myself in several religious traditions at once without having to choose between them, as if they were mutually exclusive.

During my teen years I studied the fine arts, with the mentoring of my uncle David. From 1954–58 I attended Scripps College in Claremont, California, a school that focused on the fine arts and the humanities. I began as an art major but was drawn into the classics department by a charismatic teacher, Robert Palmer. I learned Latin, Greek, French, and German, and immersed myself in the literature, history, and philosophy of ancient Greece and Rome. I investigated the ancient religious origins of Greek tragedy. From these classics studies, I became intrigued with the question of how Christianity, an unlikely apocalyptic Jewish sect, managed to gather up all of ancient culture in a new synthesis and dominate the Roman world within three centuries.

My classics teachers did not particularly appreciate Christianity. I remember Palmer saying sadly, when speaking of the neo-Platonism that the emperor Julian promoted briefly, "it had everything. Why did it lose?" Palmer thought it was rather a shame that Christianity "won." This question became mine as well, but from the other side. What was the combination of intellectual and popular power that gave Christianity the creative energy that the best of late antique thinking lacked?

My Catholic upbringing prepared me for a life of commitment, not to a narrow, constricted faith, but to an ever-broadening understanding of being a Catholic woman in times of great social change. In the early sixties, I completed a PhD in classics and early church history and theology, a field called patristics, while raising three young children with my graduate student husband, Herman Ruether. At the time, the Second Vatican Council and a vision of reform began to sweep through the church. I wrote several articles critiquing the view of sex and reproduction that underlay the Catholic anticontraceptive position. One of these became an essay in a book, *Contraception and Holiness*, that was distributed to the bishops and theologians at the Second Vatican Council.

By an extraordinary concatenation of events, the reform movement in the Catholic Church coincided with the civil rights and peace movements in the United States. In the summer of 1965 I joined a delegation to Mississippi as a volunteer in the Delta Ministry. Our delegation was housed at Beulah, a former black college campus and headquarters of the Delta Ministry. The ministry planned housing and farm cooperatives and organized voter registration to bring blacks into their full citizen rights. I worked with the Head Start program, which planted preschool education programs in black churches in poor black communities. For the first time I glimpsed the United States from the underside, from the perspective of poor, black people.

What I experienced in the Delta was dangerous and frightening. One night, hooded Ku Klux Klansmen rode through the campus, shooting randomly through the windows of the buildings. Thereafter, in case they returned, we stationed a nightly guard to ring a bell to warn the residents to get under their beds. I developed a graphic sense of living in America as a war zone, where the local police were one's enemy. That summer, social justice permanently entered my thinking and life. Such involvement in the civil rights movement prompted many of my generation to question the patterns of racism and classism in the United States, as well as its interventionist international policies that brought it into the Vietnam War. I began to write articles that merged my knowledge of the history of Christian thought with contemporary social issues.

Without realizing it, I had hit on a liberation theology method. Using a historical method that has guided much of my work since, I asked: what are the roots of an issue in Western society and culture, such as sexism or racism; how has Christianity played into justifying this problem; what are the critical traditions in Christian thought that enable us to question this issue; and how do we go about mobilizing Christian resources to overcome it? Catholic reform has continued to be a deep commitment for me, all the more so when the forces of reaction seem to have "won" in the twenty-first century. My belief is that when the "bad guys" seem to have won, you don't run. You fight harder.

CHALLENGES TO THE VATICAN

One of the greatest nineteenth- and twentieth-century challenges to Vatican authority has come from the growing feminist movement in the church. An important impetus to feminism was a new liberalism, grounded in the view that all "men are created equal." From 1850–1930 the limitations of the old American liberalism that confined the rights of "man and the citizen" to white propertied males became evident. Slavery was abolished, and women began to claim rights to property, higher education, professional employment, and the vote. Liberals believed the true and original "order of nature" was this human equality. They challenged the traditional Christian views that class, race, and gender hierarchies were the divinely founded "order of creation." This concept of the "order of creation" sanctified social hierarchies as unchangeable, rooted in "nature" and the will of God. Social reform required the overthrow of old aristocracies and new laws that guaranteed equal rights of all citizens before the law.

In the nineteenth century, official Catholicism became the foe of liberalism and the champion of the old feudal order, which it identified with Catholic society. In 1864 Pope

Pius IX issued the *Syllabus of Errors*, which condemned liberalism and socialism, decrying democracy and the freedoms of thought, press, education, and religion as modern errors. Pius IX consolidated both doctrinal and jurisdictional control over the church in the hands of the Papacy by convoking the First Vatican Council (1870), where the Pope was declared to be "infallible." Though claiming to be an ancient Catholic tradition, such an assertion of papal infallibility at this time was the Vatican's response to modern ideas seen as threatening Catholicism.

However, male liberals (not just Catholics) were mostly not open to women's rights, but reinforced male domination in political and economic affairs. The industrial revolution had shaped a new middle-class family based on the split between home and work. Paid work and politics were seen as the sphere of men, while women were to be confined to non-paid housework and child raising. Religion was privatized. Spirituality became the sphere of women and the home; secular rationality was the sphere of men in public life. Women's nature was defined as intuitive, altruistic, maternal, and non-sexual. Ideally women had no sexual feelings and endured sex for the sake of motherhood—a kind of secular Mariology.

This new ideology of family and sentimental, nonsexual womanhood was congenial in somewhat different ways to Protestantism and to Roman Catholicism. The old medieval view of woman as Eve, the inferior, disobedient sexual temptress, was muted in favor of woman's "nature" as passive, ethereal, loving, and maternal. The sexual temptress still lurked in the shadows of this definition, but she now became the "bad" woman (black or working class), or the "fallen" woman who had lost her "true" nature. Women's seclusion in the home was necessary to "protect" her from the dangers of losing her "true" nature. For Catholics, Mary was the model of the true feminine womanhood. Instead of man as superior—the norm of true humanness—and woman as defective and inferior, the new model of male-female relations was complementarity. Femininity and masculinity were seen as two "halves" of human nature, harmonized in the marital union of man and woman, but only by each sex keeping to its own distinct "nature" and sphere. Woman must not become "masculine" by acting in the public spheres, nor men "feminine" by being too much a homebody.

As the feminist movement arose in the nineteenth and early twentieth centuries, the Catholic bishops and the Vatican generally set their face against these changes, insisting that a woman's place is in the home. In 1930 Pope Pius XI condemned woman's emancipation as undermining the divinely founded obedience of the wife to her husband. Feminism was condemned as a false deflection of woman from her sole and true role as homemaker and mother (*Casti Connubii*). In the United States some prominent Catholic bishops were active in the antisuffrage movement.

However, once women won the vote, the bishops moved quickly to organize Catholic women against liberalism, socialism, and feminism. Officially recognized Catholic women's groups, such as the National Council of Catholic Women (set up in 1920), campaigned against birth control, divorce, child labor laws, and the Equal Rights Amendment.

These conservative Catholic groups championed the view that women had a totally different nature from men. Although "naturally" more spiritual, moral, and loving than men, women kept their superior nature only by maintaining their traditional roles in the home.

The Second Vatican Council (1962–65), called by Pope John XXIII, initiated a détente in the two-century battle between Catholicism and liberalism. The Declaration on Religious Liberty accepted the principle of freedom of religion and separation of church and state. This departed from the earlier Catholic insistence on Catholic states in which the Catholic Church was the sole officially recognized religion. In April 1963 the Pope issued the encyclical letter *Pacem in Terris* (Peace on Earth), which endorsed a whole gamut of civil liberties in language that echoed the American Bill of Rights. Every human person, it said, is endowed with intelligence and free will. The full and equal rights of all persons in society flow from this basic human nature. Since these rights are rooted in human nature itself, they are universal and inviolable. These rights include the right to seek truth, to freely express and communicate opinions, and to be informed about public events. The encyclical affirmed freedom of religion, of the press, of democratic assembly and participation in political life; freedom to choose one's state of life; and equal protection under the law. It also included economic rights, such as the right to a living wage, to sufficient food, to adequate housing, to medical care, to social security in sickness and old age, and to unemployment insurance.

The encyclical endorsed women's equal inclusion in

these rights of the human person in society and her entrance into public life, work, and politics. These rights were due to women simply as human persons, but their recent acceptance is the fruit of women's new consciousness: "Since women are becoming ever more conscious of their human dignity, they will not tolerate being treated as mere material instruments, but demand rights befitting a human person in both domestic and in public life" (41).

The battle of the Vatican with feminism was far from over, however, particularly as the feminist movement in the late 1960s added reproductive rights to its concerns for equal rights to education, employment, and political participation. Catholicism traditionally opposed birth control on the grounds that the only purpose of sex was procreation. This anticontraceptive tradition was shared with Protestantism. However, by the 1930–1950s mainstream Protestantism was accommodating itself to the practice of contraception. In 1930 the Anglican Communion meeting at Lambeth allowed contraception in some cases. The Vatican responded with the encyclical *Casta Connubii*, which defended the traditional view of marital sexuality, as well as condemning divorce and women's emancipation.

However, by the 1960s more and more Catholics, including moral theologians and priests, were no longer convinced by this anticontraceptive view. I published "A Catholic Mother Speaks out on Birth Control" in the *Saturday Evening Post* in 1963. During the Second Vatican Council several collections of articles were sent to the bishops arguing for reform of this view. I contributed to three of these collections: *What Modern Catholics Think of Birth Control, The Experience of Marriage: The Testimony of Catholic Laymen*, and *Contraception and Holiness.*

Pope Paul VI wanted to exclude the discussion of birth control from the council and so he set up a separate Birth Control Commission. This included demographers and sociologists as well as representatives of Catholic married couples. The result of these deliberations from 1964–68 was that most of the members of the commission were convinced that the traditional teaching should be changed. But a few moral theologians persuaded the Pope to reject the findings of the commission and reassert the traditional teaching. This appeared in July 1968 in the paper encyclical *Humanae Vitae.*

The tacit consensus in favor of this traditional teaching had been broken, however. More theologians and priests, even bishops, openly dissented from it and the Catholic laity mostly ignored it. For the first time in modern Catholic history, an official teaching of the Pope was explicitly "not received" by the majority of Catholics. Yet the Vatican has refused to mute its anticontraceptive position. Pope John Paul II (1978–2005) and Benedict XVI (elected in 2005) have continued to insist on the unchangeableness of this teaching. However, Catholic bishops in the 1980s, sensing that the birth control issue was lost and Catholic couples could not be controlled in bed, have focused on the church's prohibition of abortion. They have sought to prevent the legalization of abortion or to recriminalize it.

In the 1970s feminism was no longer simply a secular movement seeking women's vote, equal access to employment, and reproductive rights. It had also moved into the churches. Feminist theology challenged the whole tradition of women's subordination as an expression of God's "order of creation." Feminists challenged male language for God and maleness as a definition of normative humanness. Catholic women were among the leading feminist theologians in the United States and Europe. Catholic feminist theologians emerged in Latin American, Asian, and African churches as well as in the United States, and women both in religious orders and the laity articulated feminist views.

PROGRESSIVE CATHOLICISM
FOR THE WORLD

In my corpus of some forty-three books and hundreds of articles written between 1963 and 2008, I have addressed a vast array of issues that have evolved from my ecumenical upbringing, my family's international roots, and my feminist commitments not only to women's dignity and equality but also to justice for all the world's downtrodden and oppressed. I have written on the church (especially Roman Catholicism), feminism, anti-Semitism in Christianity, racism against African Americans, Latin American liberation theology, Christian theological history from women's perspective, the mistreatment of Palestinians by the state of Israel, ecology, family, and Buddhist-Christian dialogue. For me, these many issues are deeply interconnected. Most of them have been present in my thinking since the late 1960s or early 1970s. Even my earliest collections of essays, such as *Libera-*

tion Theology: Human Hope Confronts Christian History and American Power (1972), address most of them. My subsequent books on one or another of these issues represent a deepening process rather than a change of focus.

My first talk on sexism and theology, written in 1968, was entitled "Male Chauvinist Theology and the Anger of Women." I learned by giving this talk at various seminaries and churches that "anger" was expected from blacks in response to their discrimination, but taboo for women. In 1972 I was invited to be a visiting scholar at Harvard Divinity School to teach feminist theology on a leave from my appointment at Howard University School of Religion. In that year, I put together the research on the historical background of sexism in the Christian traditions from its roots in the ancient Near East to its modern expression. I was also able to explore these questions with a bright, critical group of students, many of whom have gone on to be major writers and thinkers in the field.

Sexism was only one social issue I was exploring in the fall of 1972. I also addressed anti-Semitism. My uncle David made me aware in childhood of Christian hostility to Judaism and resistant to it. At the end of World War II, newsreels about the horror of the Nazi death camps played in movie theatres and brought that reality home to my nine-year-old consciousness. In reading the writings of the church fathers, I became aware of how often the stereotypes of woman, as representative of the "bad body," coincided with that of Jews as a different kind of "bad body." I began to investigate how

Christianity split from Judaism in the first century and how it forged a polemic against Jews that would be passed down in pogroms, until it was taken over by Hitler in the twentieth century in the "final solution," the Holocaust. In 1972 I arrived at Harvard prepared to finish a book I had begun on Christian anti-Semitism and taught my research as a course that year. It was published in 1974 as *Faith and Fratricide: The Theological Roots of Anti-Semitism.* None of my feminist or social activist friends understood why I was writing on this topic. Though the connections between hatred of Jews and hatred of women and racial groups, such as African Americans, seemed obvious to me, this was not a common perception among feminists then.

Drawing connections among forms of oppression was controversial in other ways as well. In 1975 I sensed that my time at Howard was coming to an end. Young black women were coming to the seminary and wanted to add the gender issue to the mix of questions, but the rest of the faculty was extremely resistant to doing so. One young woman wrote her master's thesis on sexism in the black church and was openly ridiculed by the faculty. When I tried to defend her, the faculty attacked me as "racist." I was in a no-win situation for a white feminist at a black seminary. I decided to move on and make room for black women professors who could address this issue in the black context. In 1976 I received the offer to be the Georgia Harkness Professor of Applied Theology at Garrett-Evangelical Theological Seminary, a Methodist school on the campus of Northwestern University in

Evanston, Illinois, that was committed to dealing with both racism and sexism. Our family moved to the Chicago area so I could take this job.

At Garrett I developed my research more deeply on many of the issues I had begun to explore from 1966–76, publishing a number of books on sexism in Judeo-Christian tradition and Jewish and Christian women's leadership through the ages. Rosemary Skinner Keller, my colleague at Garrett, and I edited the three-volume series *Women and Religion in America: A Documentary History.* In 1995 we published a synthesis of these three books, together with material from 1965 to the present in one volume, *In Our Own Voices: Four Centuries of Women's Religious Writings.* Although my own studies had focused on the early centuries of the church, this work with Keller has made me something of an American women's history scholar as well. In the last ten years we edited a major three-volume encyclopedia on women and religion in America, which won the American Historical Society Award for best reference book published in 2006. Our roster of 165 contributors draws on many of the colleagues in American women's religious history we have cultivated over the years.

How had Christianity justified the exclusion of women from leadership? How has this changed over the centuries? What are the resources in the tradition for the inclusion of women? When I first began teaching feminist theology in the early 1980s, there were scarcely any resources to answer such questions. I assembled documents that showed the variety of views of gender in the ancient Near Eastern, biblical, and early Christian traditions, organized around the topics of theology: the nature of God, the trinity, creation, anthropology or human nature, Christology, church, ministry, and eschatology. I intentionally expanded these readings beyond the Christian tradition to help students see the larger context of resources for looking at gender from the ancient Near Eastern world in which Judaism was embedded. Using this set of documents, I developed a series of lectures that discussed the theological construction of these topics of systematic theology from the perspectives of women. My method involved a double approach: critiques of the patterns of exclusion and the lifting up of more inclusive traditions. These lectures were published as *Sexism and God-talk: Toward a Feminist Theology* in 1983. The set of readings came out two years later as *Womenguides: Texts for Feminist Theology.*

In the 1980s I received a number of important opportunities to develop my ideas. In 1984 some women in Sweden developed an application for a Fulbright to bring a feminist theologian to teach there and invited me. My time in Sweden was a wonderful opportunity to network with feminist women in the church in Europe and get a sense of women's issues in the European context. I gave lectures in Lund, where I was based, and additional lectures in Stockholm, Uppsala, Oslo, Copenhagen, and Arhus. I decided to focus my writing during this period on feminist liturgies and ideas of "women church" or feminist base communities.

My work on Christian anti-Semitism also was bringing invitations to speak in synagogues and in Jewish-Christian dialogue conferences. Gradually it became apparent to me that there was a political agenda behind many of these invitations that remained unspoken. Christians critical of Christian anti-Semitism were expected to commit themselves wholeheartedly to the side of the state of Israel in its conflicts with the Palestinians and the Arab world. At lectures, I was asked questions such as "why doesn't the Pope recognize the state of Israel?" Since these questions about Israel had nothing to do with my research or concerns, I was at first puzzled by such queries and commented that I was not in regular conversation with the Pope about this or any other matter. One synagogue mother came up to me after a lecture and whispered to me in a state of great agitation, "They are just using you." It became evident that there was a big gap in my understanding of the agenda behind such questions; namely, the politics of American Jews in relation to the state of Israel and the Arab world. I decided to learn something about it.

In 1980 I had a chance to travel to Israel with a group of women. The trip was organized by Jewish women from Montreal who billed it as an opportunity for dialogue and peacemaking among Jewish, Christian, and Muslim women. The hope was that somehow women might be able to talk to each other across these differences in ways that men had not. It sounded promising and I signed on. It soon became evident, however, that the trip was totally skewed toward the Israeli-Jewish view of the situation. The one Muslim woman, a Canadian originally from Egypt, dropped out when the bias of the trip became evident. There was no real effort to go to the Palestinian areas or to talk to Palestinians.

Several of us on the trip, including Charlayne Hunter-

Gault of PBS's *McNeil-Lehrer Report*, began to discuss this bias. We decided to use our free day to "slip away" from the main itinerary and to meet with Palestinians. I knew the writings of Raymonda Tawil, a Palestinian feminist journalist, and called her up. She arranged for us to come to their news office in East Jerusalem where we discovered not only Palestinian spokespeople, but Israelis critical of their government, to which we had not been exposed on our packaged tour. Raymonda arranged for us to have a quick exposure to the Palestinian reality. We met with the mayor of Ramallah, whose legs had been blown off by an Israeli bomb. We visited Palestinian women working in the famed center, In-ash el-Usra, run by the indomitable Um Khalil (later to run for president of the Palestinian Authority against Yasir Arafat), and we saw a refugee camp.

These brief, intense experiences made us deeply aware of the very different reality that lay just on the other side of the invisible line: the dispossessed Palestinians and the underside of the State of Israel. Our hosts were very upset when we returned, especially at Hunter-Gault, a prominent African American journalist whom they had hoped to influence, but they kept their anger under control. This intensified our sense that we had uncovered a secret story which we were not to know. I resolved to read more about Zionism, the history of Israel, and the Palestinian struggle.

In 1986 my husband and I took sabbatical leave to live for some months at Tantur, a Christian ecumenical study center at the checkpoint between Jerusalem and the Palestinian Occupied Territories, on the Bethlehem road. I took the opportunity to teach a class on Zionism, Israel, and the Palestinians, while my husband taught on Islam. Our stay at Tantur made us more aware of how religion and the critique of anti-Semitism was being misused simultaneously to justify the dispossession of the Palestinians and ignore their existence. We came home from the sabbatical with an outline for a book which would cover Christian, Jewish, and Islamic views on the land of Palestine and the history of the conflict between Israel and the Palestinians, with an eye to the use and abuse of religious ideology. This was published in 1989 as *The Wrath of Jonah: The Crisis of Religious Nationalism in the Israeli-Palestinian Conflict.*

The publication of this book quickly made evident what I had only suspected: namely, that Jewish-Christian dialogue was predicated on making Christians docile yea-sayers to the policies of the State of Israel, without ever naming the unjust treatment of the Palestinians. I was no longer welcomed to Jewish-Christian dialogue conferences, and invitations to speak on *Faith and Fratricide* disappeared, even though I had not changed my mind at all about the material in that book. At the same time, however, a new and more rewarding network of colleagues opened up for me: Christians, Jews, and Muslims working on justice for Palestinians in groups such as the Palestine Human Rights Campaign.

My work on Palestinian-Israeli peace and justice and the survival of Palestinian Christians in the "Holy Land" goes on primarily through the Sabeel Center, a Palestinian liberation theology center founded by Father Naim Ateek in Jerusalem, with supporting networks in Canada, the United

States, Britain, and Sweden. Jewish liberation theologian Marc Ellis was head of the Peace and Justice Center at Mary-knoll School of Theology when I first met him in the 1980s. When Maryknoll closed he found himself in a difficult struggle to find another job, given the pressure against him from the American Jewish community in response to the positions he had taken on justice for Palestinians. Finally, he was able to find both a university professorship and the base for a center on the American Jewish experience at Baylor University in Waco, Texas. The irony that only a Southern Baptist school in Texas was able to risk hiring such a controversial Jewish figure, while Christian schools on the East Coast shunned him, was not lost on us.

The situation for Palestinians, far from improving in the 1990s with the so-called Oslo peace process, has greatly worsened. My e-mail news is overwhelmed on a daily basis with stories of the latest random shooting and shelling of Palestinian neighborhoods by the Israeli army. In the summer of 2001 my husband and I committed ourselves to an update of *The Wrath of Jonah* to try to capture main outlines of this worsening history of the last twelve years. The gap between the reality of the Palestinian experience and the cover-up of that reality by the dominant media is still very large, and most Americans remain ignorant of the true story.

Feminism and feminist theology remain myopic if they are confined to white U.S. Americans. In addition to the intense and absorbing Palestinian plight, I still remain deeply involved in the international feminist theology movement. Women's theology must become multicultural and multicontextual, and this diversity includes black, Hispanic, and Asian feminist theologies in the United States. But of particular interest for me is the development of feminist theologies in Latin America, Africa, and Asia. Women from these areas began to gather from the mid-1980s to contextualize their theologies. I was privileged to be able to go to some of the international meetings of First and Third World women's theologians, as well as to travel to many Latin American countries, such as Nicaragua, Guatemala, Costa Rica, Brazil, Argentina, Chile, and Peru; to the African countries of South Africa and Zimbabwe; and to China, Japan, Korea, the Philippines, and India to meet and work with women in these many contexts. These contacts resulted in a series of books in the 1990s on women, religion, and ecology—this last subject had been a concern of mine since 1975.

I have continued to write on ecology, feminism, and the Palestinian plight. In 2005 I turned to a long-standing concern, namely, the question of American belief in its own election and exceptionalism and the way this view has fed the drive for American empire. My goal was to develop a U.S. American theology of liberation as a theology of letting go. Can we release our hold on dominating power over others and transform ourselves into one nation among others in a just, peaceful, and ecologically sustainable world? What is the mind-set that ties the United States with the imperial obsession to be "number 1," militarily and economically? What are the resources in our religious culture for "letting go" of this obsession? This work appeared in 2007 under the title of *America, Amerikkka: Elect Nation and Imperial Violence.*

My commitment as a progressive Catholic is to the wide, inclusive agenda of a liberating future for humanity and the earth. It is about helping Christians and Americans understand how we got into the horrible distortions of anti-Semitism, racism, sexism, international militarism, imperialism, and ecological devastation, so we can begin to imagine how to get out of them. My theological writings remain deeply tied to the disciplines in which I was trained at Scripps College and Claremont Graduate School in 1954–65, the history of ideas in their social context. But this trajectory of research on the history of ideas is at the same time advocacy scholarship. What resources do we have in our traditions, in those symbols that form the base of the best of our identity, that can help us transcend systems and ideologies of oppression? What will help us glimpse a better world of partnership with each other, with the earth; a partnership that might at the same time help us glimpse a more life-giving relation to God? My life has been an exploration of these crucial questions.

2

Reproductive Rights and the Vatican's "Pro-Life Ethics"

O n no other issue is the Vatican so at odds with many of its own people as on the issue of women's reproductive rights. Pope Pius XI's encyclical *Casti Connubii*, issued on December 31, 1930, sought to define once and for all official Catholic teaching on sexuality and reproduction. The Vatican encyclical reiterated the traditional teaching on sex and marriage, ruling out all forms of contraception as "intrinsically evil"—not only barrier methods of contraception but also even coitus interruptus. From the 1930s through the 1950s, the Vatican waged a crusade against contraception, going so far as to use the confessional to query penitents as to their possible use of contraception, an intrusiveness that came to be seen as characteristic of Catholicism. In the 1950s a slight amelioration of the teaching allowed abstinence during a woman's fertile time, a practice called the "rhythm method," a form, as it were, of strategic abstinence.

The official church's statement and practices were an extraordinary example of moral absolutism that went far beyond official church judgments against other "sins" that many of us might regard as far worse than using birth control. For example, it does not deem killing as intrinsically evil in every case; it accounts for mitigating circumstances such as just war and self-defense. Stealing can also be justified if there is no other way to obtain food to prevent starvation. It was as though the church's control of marital sexuality at whatever cost to women's health and well-being, as well as that of their families, had become the central article of faith and practice for Catholic Christianity. Preventing conception was defined as a greater evil than taking a human life. Why such absolutism on this matter of contraception?

As mentioned in chapter 1, in the same year as the 1930 encyclical, the Lambeth conference of the world's Anglican bishops had conceded the morality of the use of contraception within marriage. Their decision came in the wake of late-nineteenth- and early-twentieth-century public campaigns for birth control in England and the United States, healthier views of sexuality, and the development of new or better methods of contraception, such as the diaphragm, thin rubber condoms, and spermicidal jellies. Though the Anglican decision was stated in highly conservative terms, advocating abstinence as the "primary and obvious method" of contraception and allowing other methods only where this was not possible, the decision and a declining Catholic birthrate in Europe and the United States galvanized the Vatican into reaction and elevated anticontraception from a traditional but not particularly central issue of Roman Catholic moral theology to a virtual Vatican crusade against women's reproductive agency.

By 1960 the issue of contraception had become an explosive issue among Catholics. When Pope John XXIII announced his plan to assemble a council to "update" Catholicism, many reform-minded Catholics were determined that the traditional view on contraception be among the teachings to be revised. With a United Nations conference on population coming up in 1964, John XXIII wanted the Catholic Church to have a credible position. Doubts about the unchangeable infallibility of traditional Catholic teaching on the contraception issue had been spreading to leading reform bishops, such as Dutch bishop William Bekkers and Cardinal Leo Joseph Suenens of Brussels. When the council opened in 1962, Bekkers and Suenens were present in it. A conservative Franciscan theologian prepared a document for the council on marriage, *De Castitate*, that simply repeated traditional teaching. Suenens urged the Pope to form a small commission to study the birth control issue in depth and handpicked the first six members of the commission, which included a demographer, a sociologist, an economist, and two medical doctors.[1]

John XXIII died in June 1963, and his successor, Paul VI, decided to continue and enlarge the birth control commission to fifty-eight members. He included five women, gave it a majority of lay people, and appointed representatives from every continent. There were sixteen theologians, but most of the members were experts in other fields, such as doctors, psychologists, and economists. By 1964, four books testifying to views among Catholic moral theologians and married lay leaders that dissented from the Vatican had been rushed into print and circulated at the council.[2] In addition to the books, there were articles by bishops, such as Thomas Roberts, challenging the tenability of the past views and calling for reform.

The commission had three married couples, from French Canada, France, and the United States. The U.S. couple, Pat and Patty Crowley, led the international Christian Family Movement. The Crowleys solicited letters from their CFM constituents on their experiences with "natural" family planning and its effects on their sexual life and family well-being, and they took a hundred of these letters with them to report to the commission as evidence of the problems of the rhythm method. The members of the commission were aghast at the stories of suffering and hardship that they received. They heard tales of unplanned pregnancies despite careful efforts to observe the "rules." They listened to stories of economic and physical hardship and loss of health, caused by too many children closely spaced. Couples described their feelings of fear of sexuality and resentment against one another in trying to enforce the sexual regimen of periodic abstinence.

Later the Crowleys conducted a systematic survey with over three thousand respondents from eighteen countries. They received responses similar to their own experiences of ineffectiveness, anxiety, and hardship. These reports from actual married couples were all the more impressive, since they did not come from marginal or alienated Catholics but from those seeking to be the most faithful. They made a strong impact on the commission's celibate male theologians, many of whom had never heard such testimony before. The commission's doubts about the theoretical tenability of the teaching grew. The commissioners drafted a final report of their findings that said, if the general orientation of a marriage was open to reproduction, not every sexual act had to be open to procreation. Within a framework of committed love and desire for children, any method of contraception that was medically and psychologically sound and accessible to the couple was acceptable.

The commission passed its final report, "Responsible Parenthood," by a vote of 52 to 4, including sixteen bishops and cardinals who voted 9 to 4 with 3 abstentions. The commission delivered the report to the Pope Paul VI on June 28, 1966, with a pastoral introduction explaining how the church's doctrine could "develop" on this topic.[3] However, the conservative head of the Holy Office and the leader of the four who had voted against the report were determined to undermine it with the Pope. They drafted a protest called "the minority report"—a misleading name since the commission had specifically decided to submit only one final report that represented the overwhelming majority. The protest report argued that the authority of the traditional teaching was infallible.[4]

The minority protest position did not answer the arguments raised in the commission, but simply asserted the church's static, unchangeable teaching authority. They also sought to persuade the Pope that if the Catholic Church changed its teaching on this subject, it would lose all credibility as an authoritative teacher for church members. This ar-

gument was particularly persuasive for Paul VI who was
deeply worried about the question of authority. Apparently,
it did not occur to these men that *not* changing the teaching,
when it had already lost credibility with both Catholic intel-
lectuals and lay people, might cause a much greater loss of
credibility. They failed to consider that confidence in the
church's teaching authority might be restored if the official
church acknowledged its teaching could adapt to new information and social conditions.

The confrontation between these two different world-
views was made vividly clear in an exchange between the
Spanish Jesuit Marcelino Zelba and Patty Crowley at the
close of the commission. When it became evident that
the majority would recommend change, Zelba commented
that if the church changed its teachings on contraception,
"What then with the millions we have sent to hell, if these
norms were not valid." Crowley, astonished that Zelba would
see this as a problem, responded, "Father Zelba, do you really believe that God has carried out all your orders?"[5]

This exchange sums up the crux of the Vatican's problem.
The key issue for the official celibate male clerics of the
church's hierarchy was the maintenance of their unques-
tioned power to define the sexuality of lay people and to in-
voke sanctions of eternal hellfire if they did not obey. They
assumed not only that they knew God's will fully, but also that
God was an instrument of their power. They believed that
they were empowered to define sexual sin and its punishment and that God was at their disposal to carry out their orders. That their definitions may have had nothing to do

either with the realities of sexual relations or with God was obvious to Crowley but unthinkable to Zelba. The Vatican, obsessed with its own authority, still exhibits an absence of concern for the well-being of women and children.

A few men working in secret persuaded the Pope to reject the overwhelming majority opinion of his own commission and to reaffirm the traditional teaching. He stated his reactionary position in the encyclical *Humanae Vitae*, published on July 29, 1968. The majority members of the commission were shocked. Several spoke critically of the decision. Charles Curran, moral theologian at Catholic University, who had already faced down an effort to fire him for his mildly dissenting views on birth control, drafted a critique of the encyclical; six hundred Catholic theologians around the world signed it. The Vatican sanctioned any theologian who broke ranks on its teachings. Cardinal O'Boyle of Washington, DC, came down brutally on the dissenters. Curran and twenty-three other dissenters were suspended, as well as thirty parish priests; most ended up leaving the priesthood. Nonetheless, many bishops' conferences around the world responded ambivalently. Instead of endorsing the encyclical fully, they spoke vaguely of the rights of conscience for those who did not agree with it.[6]

The Vatican's betrayal of its own consultative process was disastrous for its own credibility, leading some church observers to conclude that the encyclical lacked validity because it clearly had not been "received" by the overwhelming majority of the Catholic people.[7] Many Catholic lay people decided to leave the church, but most decided that they could remain Catholics and reject this particular teaching. Regular church attendance and financial support for the church among American Catholics dropped sharply between the late 1960s and 1980s, largely due to reactions to the encyclical.[8] Subsequent polls consistently show that 80 percent of American Catholics believe they can be good Catholics and reject this teaching, which indicates a fundamental paradigm shift away from centuries of acceptance of the church's teaching authority.[9]

This overwhelming dissent did not deter Roman Catholic hardliners. They saw themselves as the "faithful remnant" that maintained the "truth" against an apostate world seeking to overtake the church. Although Paul VI remained anguished by his own decision, a Pope without doubts followed him (after the short papacy of John Paul I). The former archbishop of Krakow, Karol Wojtyla, became John Paul II in 1978. Wojtyla had actually been one of the sixteen bishops named to the birth control commission, but declined to attend. Thus, he participated in none of the conversations that led to the majority view.

John Paul II accepted completely the view that the traditional teaching was not only unchangeable but infallible and took every opportunity to extol and to enforce *Humanae Vitae*. His head of the Congregation of the Doctrine of the Faith, Joseph Ratzinger, officially stripped Charles Curran of his ecclesiastical permission to teach as a Catholic theologian in August of 1986. He now teaches at a Protestant university and seminary. In 1993, the Vatican issued a major encyclical on moral theology, *Veritatis Splendor*, which upheld the view that every act of contraception was essentially evil and that any dissent or critical discussion was disallowed. Addressing himself, not to the Catholic people, but to the Catholic bishops, the Pope decreed that no institution can be called Catholic that does not uphold this teaching, whether a school, a medical facility, or a counseling service. The strict view of contraception as intrinsically evil (along with rejection of women's ordination) became a litmus test for advancement to any leadership position in the church as bishop, seminary president, or head of a religious order. The stage was set for a full-scale purge of any dissenters in the church, particularly theologians who were also priests. The persecution also included the occasional woman religious, layman, or laywoman who held a leadership position in a Catholic institution.

Even though the vast majority of lay Catholics can dissent simply by behaving otherwise in their personal sexual lives and declining to submit to the confessional, the Catholic Church's teaching continues to have enormously deleterious effects through its influence on local national and global public policy. In many predominately Catholic countries where the Catholic hierarchy maintains a strong influence on political leaders, contraception is not readily accessible and abortion is illegal. This forces women to resort to illegal abortions with the high levels of death and injury due to unsafe conditions.

The Catholic Church maintains a virtual stranglehold on Catholic hospitals, even in countries such as the United States. The Catholic Church lobbies against family planning programs for poor women, provided through Title X of the Public Health Service Act. It is estimated that the publicly supported clinics provided by this act have helped women prevent twenty million unwanted pregnancies over the last two decades and have, thereby, greatly reduced the need for abortions. Catholic opposition means that, not only is abortion not done in many hospitals, but contraception, including emergency contraception for victims of rape or incest, is not available. Cutting insurance coverage for contraception is another area where Catholic influence has been felt in state and federal policy. U.S. policies also have a global impact. George W. Bush, seeking to "pay his dues" to Catholic as well as right-wing Protestant political support, reimposed the "global gag rule" on his first day in office in 2001. It barred any overseas family planning organization from receiving U.S. family planning funds if it supported legal and safe abortion, even if it did so with its own funds.[10]

From the first, Bush catered to the Christian right, including the Catholic right, in social policy and cabinet and judicial appointments. Attorney General John Ashcroft subpoenaed the medical records of women who had abortions and his Justice Department argued in court that the law need not honor doctor-patient confidentiality. Bush's first secretary of the Department of Health and Human Services, Tommy Thompson, opposed abortion and signed bills declaring that life began at conception. Bush also continually appointed antichoice men and women to represent the United States at international population conferences and as judges to U.S. circuit courts. Bush sought to strip contra-

ceptive coverage from the Federal Employees Health Benefit Plan.

In the meantime, the approach to population issues has
changed somewhat in the last twenty years. Many members
of the United Nations have rejected the coercive imposition
of population control and have instituted broad ethical
guidelines that empower women's education and community
health. The 1994 United Nations Cairo Conference on Population and Development declared that couples and individuals have a right to determine freely the number and spacing
of their children and to have the information and the means
to do so. The conference said women's reproductive rights
were an integral part of human rights and were a major principle in the documents of the conference.

The Vatican had no understanding of the import of these
changes. Instead it tried to appeal to a rhetoric of hostility to
Western imperialism and feminism to sway Third World and
Islamic nations against women's reproductive rights. At the
Cairo conference the Vatican sought to prevent advocacy for
any element of sex education, accessible contraception, family planning, and legal and safe abortion, in alliance with
some of the most reactionary Islamic countries, as well as a
handful of conservative representatives of Catholic states,
such as Nicaragua and Malta. Disgusted with the Vatican's
obstructionist role at UN conferences on population and development, some international NGOs, led by Catholics for a
Free Choice / Catolicas por el Derecho a Decidir, inaugu-
rated the See Change campaign to promote the idea that the
Vatican should not be represented at the United Nations as if

it were a state, but rather should be present as an NGO like any other religious organization. Although this campaign seems unlikely to succeed any time soon, it has spotlighted the disproportionate power the Vatican exercises at UN meetings.[11]

The twenty-first century has seen devastatingly reactionary trends in both global religion and politics, led by fundamentalist religions (particularly Catholic, Protestant, and Muslim). Women's reproductive rights have become one of the central targets of this unholy alliance of right-wing religion and politics. Bush reversed U.S. support for the 1994 UN Cairo agreement. Bush's antichoice Christian Right delegates to the Asian/Pacific conference on Population and Development in December 2002 tried to dismantle sex education programs, ban condom use for HIV/AIDs prevention, and block programs to prevent and treat unsafe abortions. Bush has continually supported "abstinence only" sex education policies and appointed representatives that promote these policies as the only acceptable form of family planning. This has also been applied to HIV/AIDs funding. Patricia Funderburk Ware, who supports an "abstinence only" policy to prevent HIV/AIDs, was appointed to head the presidential advisory committee on HIV/AIDs. This policy has also been applied to U.S. funding for AIDs prevention in Africa. In March of 2003 U.S. funding for AIDs prevention in Africa, promised in Bush's State of the Union address in January of that year, was effectively gutted by applying the global "gag rule" to these funds. No agency that receives funds from the United States can counsel on abortion or contraception, including the use of condoms as a method to avoid contracting AIDs. Two hundred million dollars were cut from funding programs for women's reproductive health in Afghanistan, and three million in aid for the World Health Organization was frozen to prevent research on mifpristone, an emergency contraception pill that prevents the implantation of a fertilized egg.[12]

The Vatican's role in the global tragedies of untimely death is grounded in its moral contradictions. Despite its claim to a "consistent life ethic," the official church uses very different kinds of moral reasoning when it comes to questions of war than when it deals with abortion. This contradiction was pointed out in 1988 by Catholic ethicist Christine Gudorf.[13] She noted that Vatican ethics uses an absolutist version of natural law ethics when it speaks of abortion, asserting one value above all others. It allows no debate, applies coercive sanctions and excommunication, and demands criminalization. Yet, when the Vatican speaks of war, it shifts to a consequence-based ethic that carefully balances conflicting values. For war, it draws on a multiplicity of perspectives, allows for various opinions, relies on persuasion, not legal sanctions, and ultimately leaves matters in the hands of individual conscience. Where is the bishop who would say that soldiers who directly massacre noncombatant civilians are to be excommunicated? Where are bishops who would suggest that those who manufacture nuclear weapons are excommunicated and should repent by leaving such forms of employment? Some years ago, two Mexican bishops declared that torturers were excommunicated, but they were maverick leftists. Neither their fellow bishops nor the Vatican supported their views. In short, official Catholicism speaks softly and carries no stick when it comes to untimely and unjust death *after* birth.

The official church makes absolute the right to life of the unborn, even of fertilized eggs in the first days after conception, but it possesses little moral rigor when it comes to the vast carnage of human beings between birth and old age from war, poverty, and environmental devastation. While Catholicism theoretically forbids the direct taking of innocent life at any stage of life, it applies the most rigorous sanctions to taking unborn life, while it applies no sanctions to killing noncombatants in war, selling toxic waste to farmers as fertilizer, favoring military spending over social welfare spending, impoverishing the poor and favoring their exploitation by the rich and their corporations, or any number of other actions that have the consequences of unjust and untimely death. Only unborn life, it appears, is really "innocent" and worthy of moral protection.

The Vatican ignores other options in Catholic tradition in taking its position. An alternative tradition does not teach that a "human person" is present from the first moment of conception. Catholicism follows this alternative view in its pastoral practice, as is evident from its refusal to baptize even late-term miscarriages. Traditionally, Catholicism has viewed human nature as an integral union of body and soul. It has taught that the human soul is present only when the body of the fetus has achieved a certain level of human physical development, usually at about five months. Today we might see this as the point where brain development reaches the level of sustaining human life outside the womb. Despite Vatican rhetoric, the Catholic tradition has never actually taught that human life begins at conception.[14]

Although a fertilized egg has a different ethical status from a person already born, it is not "nothing." Rather it is a potential life that is in the process of actualization, and abortion should be "legal, safe and rare," as President Bill Clinton noted. In a few, relatively rare situations, an abortion is decided because the fetus is severely deformed, carries a serious genetic malady, or threatens the life of the mother. Most abortions occur, however, because the pregnancies are unintended. We know that women's social, economic, and cultural situations in male-dominant systems throughout the world mean that women often do not choose the conditions under which they have sex, even in marriage. Women are frequently coerced into having sex, while not having control of its results. Even when women want to use contraception, men often do not cooperate. For such reasons, as well as rape and sexual abuse, women find themselves involuntarily pregnant. Although many women are able to adjust to unintended pregnancies, many others feel deeply threatened by a situation in which, psychologically, socially, and/or economically, they are not in a position to bear and raise a child. Their situation is only worsened by coercive legal measures, such as criminalizing abortion. Such measures will only assure that abortion becomes clandestine, unsafe, and more likely to result in the deaths or injuries of the women, as well as making her a criminal.

In El Salvador, an Opus Dei archbishop and a campaign by right-wing Catholics has resulted in a national law criminalizing all abortions. The result has been a large number of clandestine abortions, mostly by poor women (since the wealthy can get abortions from private doctors or in other countries). Many have died or been injured. When they go to hospitals or otherwise seek medical care, they are taken into custody and can be imprisoned. The penalty for the abortion provider is 6–12 years, anyone who helps the women can receive 2–5 years, and sentencing for the woman herself is 2–8 years for the first trimester and 30–50 years thereafter. One desperately poor mother who aborted an eighteen-week fetus was imprisoned for thirty years, even though her three small children were dependent on her as their sole parent. Absolutizing the life of the unborn and disregarding the lives of the born affects not only the woman, but all those around her.

Catholic ethics must recognize that the decision for or against abortion involves conflicting values of life. It is not simply a matter of the "murder of innocent life" as if there were no values of life on the other side that are equally or more imperative in particular contexts. In the case of the Salvadoran woman, she was caught in desperate circumstances of poverty and chose survival for herself and her three children for whom she was the sole provider rather than bearing yet another child she could not afford to support. Women are caught in such conflicting situations where their ability to function economically, psychologically, and socially has to be weighed against the value of a potential child.

The Vatican's contradictory religious ethic denies women effective birth control and disparages women's moral agency, making the Catholic Church a major force in the world that causes some women to need abortions. Abortions should be reduced as much as possible, but not by coercing women to bear children they feel they cannot bear. Rather women should be helped as much as possible to avoid unintended pregnancy in the first place. This is the issue "pro-life" advocates avoid because it is a very complex problem and cannot be reduced to an absolute, single principle. It requires making effective and safe contraception readily accessible. But it also means addressing all the cultural issues that put women in the position of being coerced into sex, that deny them adequate sex education to avoid pregnancy, and, above all, do not grant them full moral agency to enforce their preferences about sex and birth control. In sum, official Catholicism both forbids abortion under any circumstances and is a major cause of producing the situations that cause it.

The Vatican seems to be fixated on seeking to return women to passive acquiescence to male domination while absolutizing the lives of embryos. In my view, this does not mean that embryos or fetuses have no value, but these states of life must be appropriately balanced in relation to the enormous threats to those already born. Official Catholic ethics needs to attend to the decisions of women to have or not have children. It would be far more principled in defending life if it included life *after* birth and condemned those whose policies are causing untimely death through war, environmental devastation, and economic exploitation.

A "consistent life ethic" is a nice slogan. But what would it mean in Catholic ethical teachings and practice? It means, most importantly, Catholics must be willing to trust women to make the decision that is best for them in sexual and reproductive matters, precisely what the Catholic Church's hierarchy has been least willing to do. Catholics should recognize the need for effective, affordable birth control. Moreover Catholics must be willing to help provide support services that would lessen conflicts that are at the root of women's problems with raising unexpected children. In other words, how might we help relieve the distresses that cause a woman to make a decision that she might prefer not to make in better circumstances? We can help a woman find adequate medical care, a better job, and affordable day care for her children.

Affirming the ethic of life both before birth and after birth would help overcome the credibility gap from which Catholic teachings on ethics presently suffer. Only by putting these two ethics more in sync with each other can we genuinely speak of a "consistent life ethic." The official church does not have a pro-life ethic, but uses the term as code for an absolutist rejection of both contraception and abortion under any circumstances, while it ignores the myriad threats to human life after birth.

With the election of Joseph Ratzinger as Pope Benedict XVI there seems little hope for rethinking the official church's disastrous policies. Ratizinger was John Paul II's hatchet man, and he enforced reactionary views against contraception and abortion. There is little doubt that Ratzinger adheres to the view that contraception is intrinsically evil in every instance, even in marriage. While rigidly judgmental about the sexuality of lay people, Ratzinger protects sexually abusive priests. In a confidential letter to all Catholic bishops, Ratzinger ordered that church investigations into priests accused of sexually abusing children should be kept secret, to prevent such allegations from being taken up by courts of law.[15]

The Vatican's denial of reproductive agency to women is one of the most egregious forms of violence against women and children. Forced pregnancy causes millions of deaths, physical injuries, and loss of health, and it impairs human development. When denied the moral right and the ability to choose sex and pregnancy, women are continually threatened with injury and death, and the lives of their families are at risk of poverty and/or the loss of maternal care. In addition, having to submit to unwanted sex and unintended pregnancies prevents women's educational development and capacity to live full lives. Children are also denied the necessity of being wanted, welcomed, and loved. The world's increasingly scarce environmental resources and ecological well-being are threatened by overpopulation. In the face of these disastrous consequences, the official church insists on the passive acceptance of pregnancy and child bearing as woman's "natural" fate and duty. The Vatican has been and continues to be the primary source of shaping and enforcing this violence against women, and this connivance with violence undermines its authority and its claims to value life.

3

Good, Evil, and the Church's Mission

Progressive Catholics have often been accused by those who fancy themselves as "orthodox Catholics" of a "cafeteria Catholicism." The implication is that progressive Catholics choose among a variety of views according to our subjective tastes, rather than embracing the fullness of the church's teachings on all subjects. Thus we are pleased when the Pope and bishops strongly oppose war and condemn the war in Iraq as lacking a basis in the just-war teachings of the church, but we decline to obey the church's teachings against birth control and continue to press for the ordination of women in spite of the Pope's insistence that church teachings always and forever forbid women's ordination.

Confidence in the teaching authority of the Magisterium, represented by the Pope and bishops, has become ever more confused in recent years with the revelations of massive sexual abuse of minors by priests and even bishops, and the way these have been covered up by bishops. How can anyone have any confidence in the teaching authority of bishops, when they themselves are in such flagrant violation of their own ethics? Lay people have continually been given the impression that illicit sexuality is the most heinous of sins, and yet we see here the way in which bishops have cut a great deal of slack for members of the clerical club in regard to sexual abuse, both for their own priests and for their system of power.

On the other hand, many lay people are not convinced that practicing artificial birth control is wrong in the context of a faithful, loving marriage that has already produced or intends to produce children. Using periodic abstinence to prevent conception rather than medically approved barrier methods or pills does not strike most Catholics as a significant difference, when the end result is the same. Certainly a distinction cannot warrant the difference between acceptable morality and deadly sin. Such Catholics wonder if a celibate clergy has any clue what married people go through when they desperately need to prevent additional births for financial or health reasons and yet lack effective methods of doing so.

By the same token, many lay Catholics, women and men, suspect that rejecting women's ordination in principle is really based on a view that women are inferior and lack full humanity. Those of us with a little historical education know that, in fact, women's ordination was traditionally rejected in the Catholic tradition on the basis of the Aristotelian view that women lacked full humanity and so could not represent Christ and could not exercise authority in society, a view based on a faulty biology that Catholicism today no longer uses as the official basis of this teaching. Thus the claim of the hierarchy that rejecting women's ordination is not a justice issue lacks credibility.

On the other hand, when neoconservative Catholic Michael Novak rejected the clear consensus of the Pope and the American and world bishops that the war in Iraq lacked a basis in the just-war tradition and should be opposed, progressive Catholics are likely to feel that we have both truth and church authority on our side. When Novak went to Rome to present his view directly to the Vatican to persuade them to endorse the war in Iraq, we rather longed to see him firmly condemned in those sacred precincts. Progressive Catholics were pleased when a major group of American Catholic leaders wrote a formal protest against Novak's views, condemning him as a "dissenting theologian" who did not represent church teaching on questions of war and peace. Is this a little contradictory?

The presumption of neoconservative Catholics, such as Novak, is that if you are a Catholic, you have to accept the whole package of the church's teachings. You cannot "pick and choose." Yet these same so-called traditionalists declined to accept the judgment of the Pope and the bishops that the war in Iraq violated the just-war teachings of the church and that the use of nuclear weapons is incompatible with the teachings on proportionality, which is the heart of the just-war tradition. Strong messages of social justice and concern for the poor also do not go down well with these "conservatives." It appears that both groups of Catholics, progressive and conservative, "pick and choose" what teachings they follow. So what is the difference? Is there a solid basis for one set of choices rather than another or is it all just arbitrary, personal preferences?

Given that it appears everyone picks and chooses, not all choices are equal. Let's consider an analogy. If you are in a cafeteria and see someone in the cafeteria skipping vegetables, salads, and fresh fruit and choosing rolls and butter, fried potatoes, and cream pies, you might think that such a person lacks principles of healthy eating. Even choices in a cafeteria should not be simply impulsive. They need to be guided by the norms of a nutritious diet. Such norms are established by the very nature of our bodies and their well-being.

By the same token, which ideas and church teachings one chooses to imbibe and which ones one leaves aside in the smorgasbord that is contemporary Catholicism is not merely arbitrary and subjective. For progressive Catholics, it is guided by norms we have developed for ourselves in our communities of reference about what are the authentic and important values of the gospel and what are not. These values have something to do with our vision of who Jesus is for us, what the church is called to be, and what its redemptive mission in history is all about.

What I wish to do here is to lay out a vision of the gospel and the mission of the church that I think guides progressive Catholicism and does indeed provide norms by which we choose among contradictory messages, not arbitrarily or merely by personal whim, but by a coherent sense of what is compatible with that vision and what is not. In other words, I would like to give us the courage of our convictions that our choices about what is believable and worthy of our commitment and what is not are conscientious decisions, rooted in some solid principles.

What is the gospel? We define the gospel as the "good news." What is it "good news" about? The Gospel of Luke defines this in terms of Jesus' first sermon to his hometown folks in Nazareth, in which he proclaimed:

> The Spirit of the Lord is upon me because he has anointed me to preach good news to the poor. He has sent me to proclaim release to the captives, the recovering of sight to the blind, to set at liberty those who are oppressed. (4:18)

Jesus proclaimed and represented the good news, which he defined as centrally about a new reign of justice on earth, one in which the poor have hope to overcome their misery, those unjustly imprisoned are released, and those oppressed by all forms of misery and injustice are liberated from their oppression.

If Jesus made social justice central to his definition of the good news, can we do less? To be Christians is precisely to be followers of Jesus, the Christ. We are called to be the ones who continue his proclamation of the good news and live this proclamation in our personal and communal lives.

THE CHURCH'S MISSION

The mission of the church is to follow Christ in proclaiming the good news, to be the place where truth is told, where the unseeing have their eyes opened to reality, and where oppression and injustice are overcome and a reign of peace and justice is established among humans and with the earth. The church's mission is to be a community of liberation, a redemptive community where one has a taste of what the world would be like if all forms of evil were overcome. This mission can never be complete and final within the finite conditions of history, but the church must be a place where humanity is moving in the direction of redeemed and redemptive living. Above all, the church should not be a place where new evils are constructed, perpetuated, and justified!

True, we are human. We all fall into sin, we continue to perpetuate problems, but at the very least the church needs to be a place where such dangers of sinfulness are acknowledged, where the community of Christ's good news knows how to critique its own failings, and repent of them. The worst contradiction to the church's mission is not primarily that members, or even the institution, at times sin, but rather that we justify such sins, that we cling to them, that we refuse to name these failings as failings, and that we refuse to repent. Refusal to repent, not only as individuals, but also as church is for me the primary sin against the Holy Spirit.

THE NECESSITY OF REPENTANCE

For me this raises the question: is any doctrine of the church's infallibility compatible with the gospel and the nature of the church and its mission? If infallibility means the church as an official institution cannot err, then it also means that the church cannot acknowledge that it has erred. Or, as the slogan on a popular T-shirt puts it, "infallibility means

never having to say you're sorry." A church that refuses to realize that it must, not only occasionally, but continually, repent of its failings, cannot put itself back on the right track. It
cannot truly proclaim the good news with credibility or man-
ifest redemptive community.

Repentance cannot be undertaken simply in terms of
generalities and abstractions; it must address the specifics of
how we have failed, as church, in concrete contexts. Bishops
need to stand in front of their people and say, "we have failed
to deal adequately with this matter of sexual abuse by priests.
We have covered it up. We have refused to listen to the cries
of victims. We have protected abusers. We have sent priests
to other church communities without informing them of the
history of such priests. We are sorry; we have a 'firm purpose
of amendment.' We are putting these specific policies in
place to rectify these situations. We have consulted with lay
people, including victims, about these policies, and we want
your feed back on them." Such repentance and truth-telling
might approximate what it means to be the church.

In order to approach this question of repentance in some
depth, we must first ask how we know what is evil. On what
basis do we judge something as evil and thus as something
from which we need to repent? The scriptures start off with a
vision of God's creation as essentially good. Light and dark-
ness, sky and earth, waters and land, birds, fish, and animals,
humans as male and female, all this diversity of God's creation is all essentially "very good." Goodness is our true nature. Evil is not.

What then is evil? How does it come about? What is its

nature and source? The Christian tradition has insisted that evil comes about, not from God's will, but from our perverted will. We turn against God and seek our own power and pleasure in a way that violates the harmony of God's creation. But evil in itself has no substance, no nature of its own. As Augustine put it, it is privation, absence of good, not a something in itself. It is not caused by anything else. It is never a rational choice, although it may be rationalized. It is always a choice against our true nature and well-being. This means that evil is not located in any form that is essential to being. It is not our feelings and passions, against our intellect. It is not a substance located in our bodies or our souls, our feeling, or our intellect. It is not our sexuality, over against our rationality. Some people, such as women or people of darker skin, are not more prone to it than others, such as lighter-skinned males. By the same token, lighter-skinned males are not, by nature, more prone to evil than women and blacks.

For me, this is best expressed by speaking of evil, not as a substance located in our bodies, our souls, our feeling, or our intellect. Rather, evil lies in the distortion of relationships, relationships among different aspects of ourselves and among different individuals and groups in relation to one another. What makes for good is right relation. Right relation means relating to different parts of ourselves and one another in a way that is not only equal, but mutually enhancing, that contributes to our mutual well-being. We not only have to give our bodies, our sexuality, our desires for pleasure and feelings their due. We need to relate mind and body, intellect and feelings in a way that is mutually enriching. Sickness is caused when we glut ourselves on pleasure in a way that is unhealthy for the body or when we deprive others of what they need for their basic nourishment. Also sick are those who starve or beat their bodies in the name of an intellectuality or spirituality cut off from its relationship to sensuality.

This understanding of goodness as mutually enhancing relationality and evil as distorted relationality also applies to our relation to one another, both individually and as groups. The underlying assumption here is that all human beings are fully human, and all humans have the capacity for fullness of life. There may be individual differences in talents and group differences in culture, but none of these differences means that some people are primarily somatic and others primarily mental or spiritual. Christianity is stunningly universalist. We believe that we all come from a common pair of ancestors and are part of the same family. We are all equally redeemable. Whenever we are tempted to define one group of people as primarily capable only of sexual reproduction and bodily labor, while others specialize in rationality and the capacity to rule over others, we violate the fundamental basis of right relationship to one another.

Whenever we construct theories that some groups of people have a different nature from others and therefore should be excluded from certain human aspirations, such as education and leadership, and should be confined to bodily labor, we are in the process of creating wrong relationship to each other. Such ideologies typically spring up when wrong relationship is already being established. Some groups of people are being exploited to do the work, so others can benefit from their work and monopolize power, wealth, and rule. The insistence that those who are being set aside for exploitation can do nothing other than these menial tasks because that is their "nature" is always a rationalization or justification of an existing injustice. This system of exploitation is what is meant by sin or social evil.

This does not mean that everyone has to do the same jobs, but rather that all jobs need to be honored as equal in dignity and also in their ability to sustain an adequate life. Some work should not be seen as so inferior that it should be treated as demeaning and paid so poorly that people who do it live on the brink of starvation, while other work is seen as so superior that it deserves to be rewarded with vast power and hundreds of times more wealth because the people who do it are vastly more important. All jobs deserve what Catholics have called a "living wage," not to be confused with a minimum wage, which in the United States is not a living wage.

There are three dimensions of the shaping of wrong relationship. The first is the fundamental acting out of the impulse to set ourselves up as those with power, wealth, and honor, by subjugating and exploiting others and forcing them into roles from which we benefit at their expense. The second dimension is institutionalizing this wrong relationship, embedding it in laws, social policies, and economic systems. The third dimension is to construct ideologies that justify such wrong patterns of relationship, declaring them to be the order of nature and the will of God. The second and third dimensions ratify the claim that there are fundamental differences of human nature between "us" and "them" and

set up institutions to socialize each generation into these unjust views. This systematizing of evil or wrong relationship is
what we might call "inherited evil." It means that we are born
into social systems already biased by sexism, racism, religious
prejudice, and class hierarchy, and we are socialized to assume that this is normal, natural, and divinely mandated.

The good news is that these systems of distortion and violence are not normal, natural, and divinely mandated. They
are wrong. They violate each of our capacities to be fully
human, those on top as well as those on the bottom. Moreover, God opts for the oppressed. God takes the side of those
who have been violated and proclaims their liberation. That
is the essence of Jesus' proclamation of the good news in his
sermon in Luke. Good news to the poor is, in one sense, bad
news to the rich. But this is in the context of a distorted system in which God judges unjust wealth and exploitation as
wrong. The proclamation also calls for the redemption of
those who are presently rich and powerful, who benefit by
injustice. Their redemption involves renouncing their unjust
wealth and power. If the poor need to be liberated from unjust poverty, the rich need to be divested of their unjust
wealth. This divestment does not mean that we reverse the
present distorted system, making the presently oppressed
oppressors. It means we seek to build a new system where
there is neither oppressed nor oppressors, but, in the words
of the American creed, there is "liberty and justice for all."
Or, to put it another way, we all flourish by enhancing one
another.

The transformation of our relationships from distorted

violence and exploitation to mutually enhanced well-being is the essence of what it means to repent, to be redeemed. This redemptive repentance is a restoration of our original true natures. Our creation in original goodness has never disappeared or been totally destroyed, but it has been distorted and violated by wrong relationship. It is restored through repentance. Such redemptive repentance also gives us a glimpse of what we call the "Reign of God," God's world as God created it to be and calls it to be.

The life and mission of the church is to be that place and that community of people where repentant transformation is continually taking place. We discover and discover again what transforming repentance means in the context of our concrete recognition of particular cases of how we have distorted our relation to ourselves and to one another. Church is not a place of perfect saints, but a place where we acknowledge our distortions so that we might relax our grip on them. Then we are able to glimpse and taste right relation, our true humanity, our true nature and goal.

The church must be the place where truth is spoken. Every church should have a sign over its front door, "truth can be spoken here." Unfortunately this is hardly the case. People think they should don the face of respectability when they go to church. Too often church is the place where people go to be comforted and lulled to sleep so members can resist knowing about the realities that distort and harm life. If a husband is an alcoholic, if a wife is being beaten, if children are drug addicts, we often try, at all costs, to prevent those we see at church from knowing of our troubles. Like a beaten wife who puts on makeup to cover up her scars, we too often think that church is a place to put on a duplicitous face, not a place where we can be truthful about ourselves and seek help from others.

This is why the revelations of sexual abuse and, especially, the bishops' cover-up of it were so shocking. Suddenly we were confronted publicly and massively with the sick side of a celibate culture. We could see how those who claimed to be our pastors perpetuated this evil year after year. Since the bishops themselves refused to deal with the problem, when victims and their advocates complained to them, the only way to force a response was to resort to the secular courts. But secular courts do not deal with sin. They deal with crime and civil damage suits. So resorting to secular courts meant that the way to deal with abusive priests and their institutional protection was to charge them with crime, send them to jail, and extract monetary payment from the church to compensate for emotional and physical injury.

I am not saying that these responses do not have their place, but they fall well short of what the church should be doing and how we should be relating to each other as church. The church as a redemptive community means a community where healing of victims takes place. It is also a place for the healing of victimizers. Removing an abuser from priestly office, putting him in therapy, finding a job for him where he has no access to children may all be appropriate actions. Throwing him out of the community where he is never again to be seen by those who now know his sins is not.

The church's treatment of abusive priests remains sub-

Christian so long as it stays on the level of punishment for crime and extraction of monetary payment for compensation of injuries. In fact, the emphasis on civil damage suits has quickly led to new abuses in which lawyers get involved for monetary reward and people are tempted to make up or fantasize about abuse that did not actually take place. There have been too many cases of these wrongful accusations.

I do not say this as someone who does not have full sympathy for victims. I have had some experience of sexually abusive priests myself. Rather, I am suggesting that we need to go to a deeper level in our response to such abusers. They should personally repent and apologize to those they have abused. They should stand before the church community and confess their sins, indicating their strong desire to heal themselves and ask for forgiveness. The people should deal with them as they deal with other pathological members of their own family, like a chronic alcoholic. They force them to confront their problems. They help keep them from "occasions of sin," a good old Catholic idea appropriately used here. They support their rehabilitation precisely by keeping them connected with the community and setting parameters and expectations on their behavior.

Bishop Rembert Weakland of Milwaukee did this when his own sexual and financial misdeeds were exposed. His way of doing so suggested something less than innocence on the part of the man who claimed to have been victimized. But Weakland did not justify himself by claiming he himself had been taken advantage of. He stood before his community and confessed. He retired from his job as bishop of Milwaukee, *into* his Benedictine community, there to spend the rest of his life dealing with his own soul among those he could count on to help him.

Monastic communities have reacted this way when such problems have been revealed in their midst. They have said, yes, we take this person out of jobs where he has access to vulnerable youth. Yes, we put him in counseling. No, we do not throw them out of the community. They are sinners, and they are our brothers. If they remain among those who know them, love them, and can help them to amend their lives, they have some hope of healing their souls. This maintaining of relation and accountability comes closer to what it means to be church than the discourse we have had so far about clergy sexual abuse that has focused on crime, punishment, and monetary compensation.

Where are we, then, as church, as followers of Christ, here in the Catholic Church of North America? We need a deep probing of the sick culture of sexual repression and covert sexual exploitation in the Catholic tradition generally, not only that of the clergy. It is time to call for an end to mandatory celibacy for the clergy and for the ordination of women and of married people. Mandatory celibacy was a mistake from the beginning. The Eastern church has known better. It retains the earlier church tradition in which celibacy is related to monastic vocation, and the ordinary clergy are married. The Western tradition made a mistake in the eleventh century in imposing celibacy on all clergy, and it has been an ongoing disaster. The reformers of the sixteenth century called for its revision, something Rome has tragically not been able to heed. So now we have to deal with the legacy of this mistake in the twenty-first century. It is high time to do so. Not, of course, that married clergy will end sexual misconduct. Married people also are capable of this. But at least it will broaden the range of people from which we draw our clergy, rather than limiting it solely to males willing to be officially celibate.

We need a more democratic church, a church where the laity participates in church governance on every level. Contrary to claims about tradition, there is nothing in the nature of the church that calls for a patriarchal hierarchical structure. This structure is simply the reflection of the social systems in which the Catholic Church was shaped by its history within the Roman empire, feudalism, and early modern European monarchies. These political contexts have nothing to do with the message of Christ. On the contrary, if we are serious about the church as a redemptive community, then a participatory democracy is much more in keeping with its mission and message.

Most of all, as Christians in the United States we need to struggle against our own society, a society which is racist, which is deeply divided between a wealthy elite and a large impoverished class, disproportionately people of color. We have to deal with the way U.S. society is the center of a world economic and military system that is monopolizing the resources of the whole earth for a small wealthy elite and unleashing enormous violence upon the whole planet, especially upon the poorer nations. We have to see how this violence is being promoted by the most bloated military budget and arsenal in the world. We need to recognize how the rest of the world increasingly sees the United States as the center of an oppressive empire.

How do we speak prophetically as followers of a Christ who announces good news to the poor, the liberation of the oppressed in the context of our society today? How do we withdraw from our own complicity with this evil system and begin to cooperate with many other concerned people around the world to build more just and sustainable social order? These are the questions that we need to ask about the church today. These questions and quests are not based on arbitrary likes and dislikes. They are grounded in the very foundations of what it means to be Christians, to be followers of Jesus, the Christ, the one who preached good news to the poor, the liberation of the oppressed, and the redemption of humanity and of the whole creation.

4

Women-Church

One of the thorniest problems for the Vatican and one on which it is most recalcitrant is the status of women in the Roman Catholic Church. In 1972, the U.S. Leadership Conference of Women Religious endorsed feminism as a critical perspective for the reexamination of the status of women religious in the church and for their justice work in society. The Leadership Conference represented 90 percent of Catholic women's communities. The Vatican decided these Catholic nuns were in dangerous revolt against their traditional roles in the church. The official church has since continued to make vigorous efforts to reassert control over women religious. One example of this is its insistence that religious orders of women submit their constitutions to the Holy See for censorship.

The Vatican seeks to restore traditional hierarchical relations to the church's Magisterium (teaching authority) and to reassert the authority of superiors over members within each religious order. It opposes democratic processes in the polities of these religious congregations. It has sought to exclude women religious from membership in their congregations if they publicly dissent on birth control or abortion. The result has been a running battle between the Vatican and many women's religious orders, with the Vatican trying to impose obedience to its demands and many religious congregations seeking to evade these demands and shelter members who fall under attack. This conflict has meant Catholic nuns have become some of the most important advocates of progressive Catholicism.

The women-church movement in Catholicism, a gathering of nuns and laywomen, reflects the volunteerism and democratic impulse of Americans to organize movements to oppose injustices, rather than passively accepting them. It also reflects the new wave of feminism that began in American society in the late 1960s, inspired by the civil rights movement. In 1968, several sisters, such as Marjorie Tuite, formed the National Assembly of Women Religious (NAWR), later renamed the National Assembly of Religious Women (NARW), to commit women in religious orders to grassroots social justice ministry, including issues of women. A year later, Margaret Traxler formed a parallel organization with women's concerns on their agenda, the National Coalition of American Nuns.

Feminists took a critical look at the supports for sexism in the Bible and theology, and sought to reshape ministry and theological education. Women from many religious traditions also organized their own worship groups, which were related to their heritage but independent of its official leadership. The Protestant feminist movement had its expression in the churches with the call for women's ordination in the Episcopal and Southern Baptist churches, and other churches which had not yet begun to ordain women, and for an end to sexual discrimination in church practices.[1] For American Catholics this new wave of feminism in society and the churches coincided with the Second Vatican Council's call for church renewal. Catholic women began to shape their own feminist movement, expecting that the changes going on in Protestant churches and theological schools— the ordination of women, feminist theology, inclusive language in liturgy, and recognition of women's reproductive rights—would reshape Roman Catholicism as well.[2]

In the same period, the Grail, a movement of lay women that originated in Holland, began to adopt a feminist agenda and to explore its meaning for their identity and work. Beginning in 1970 the Grail offered feminist conferences to the general public. Recognizing the growing number of women, Catholic and Protestant, who were studying theology in seminaries either for ordained ministry or teaching, the Grail brought this rising generation of women teachers and students in seminaries together in its center in Loveland, Ohio, to discuss what feminist theology might mean.[3]

Other Catholic feminist organizations arose in the early 1970s. In 1972 in New York City a small group of pro-choice Catholics formed Catholics for a Free Choice (CFFC) to counteract the Catholic Church's campaign against legalized abortion, which had just been won by the Supreme Court decision, *Roe v. Wade.* In 1976 CFFC founded a second branch to do lobbying on abortion in Washington, DC. By 2007 it had grown into an organization with eighteen staff in Washington, a three-million-dollar budget, and seven affiliated organizations in Latin America, one in Canada, and one in Spain, an active group in Europe that participates in the European Parliament, as well as contact groups in Poland, the Philippines, and elsewhere. In Chicago Donna Quinn founded Chicago Catholic Women in 1974 to organize around justice for women in the church, including the demand for ordination.[4]

WOMEN'S ORDINATION

A central point of conflict between lay and religious Catholic feminists and the Vatican is women's ordination. In 1975 the American Episcopal Church voted to ordain women, much to the Vatican's alarm.[5] Catholic authorities consider the Episcopal Church as belonging to the inner circle of "separated" churches, a special category of churches with possible claims to apostolic succession (even though the Vatican continues to reject the validity of Anglican orders). Hence Episcopal Church actions tend to evoke an official Catholic response, while the Vatican ignores other Protestant denominational changes.

In November of 1975, a group of women's religious orders sponsored a conference "Women in Future Priesthood Now—a Call for Action," held in Detroit, Michigan. The planners had expected a maximum attendance of six hundred. The applications moved past a thousand, and they finally closed registration at twelve hundred. The conference was organized around a two-sided demand: the admission of women to all ordained ministries and the renewal of the

church and its ministry. The speakers at the Detroit conference reflected a new generation of Catholic theologically
trained feminists who continue to shape Catholic feminism
to the present. After this successful conference it was decided to establish the Women's Ordination Conference
(WOC) as a national organization.[6]

The emphasis on women's ordination in the context of
church renewal signaled that the conference organizers did
not simply want to include women in the present model of
patriarchal clericalism; they wanted to transform the church.
They wanted a more democratic, participatory community in
which the clergy would be animators of the ministry of the
people, rather than being rulers over them as a superior
caste. Only within such renewal of community ministry
could or should women assume their place in ordained ministry. How to understand the relation between these two demands for ordination and church renewal would remain an
area of tension within the Women's Ordination Conference
to the present.

The Vatican response to the Episcopal vote, as well as to
the growing women's ordination movement among Catholic
women, was the 1976 "Declaration on the Question of the
Admission of Women to the Ministerial Priesthood." It asserted that women could not be ordained because women's
very nature as females disqualifies them. The document
claims that the church's refusal to ordain women is not a matter of social discrimination against women and that the
Catholic Church fully accepts women's civil rights in society.
However, the church cannot ordain women because the na-

ture of priesthood is incompatible with women's nature. This ban, the document insisted, is divinely founded and unchangeable. The declaration gives three main reasons for this position: 1) Jesus intentionally did not include women in ordained ministry; 2) the church's continuous (and hence infallible) tradition has excluded women from ordination; and 3) the priest represents Christ, a male. The maleness of Christ is not simply a social accident, but intrinsic to the representation of Christ (who represents God the Father). To ordain women would be to violate the sacramental affinity between Christ, God, and maleness.

The declaration does not cite as a reason to exclude women from ordination the thirteenth-century Thomistic view that women are naturally defective and lack the capacity to exercise any social leadership. This argument is no longer tenable now that the church has conceded, for the most part, civil rights for women in secular society. Instead, the declaration focuses on the sacramental relation of maleness and Christ, claiming that "there would not be this natural resemblance which must exist between Christ and his minister if the role of Christ was not taken by a man. . . . For Christ himself was and remains a man" (5:27).

Catholic theologians and biblical scholars released a storm of criticism of this document. Some, such as the eminent Karl Rahner, even suggested that this literalism about Christ's maleness was heretical. Polls showed that the number of U.S. Catholics who supported women's ordination expanded after the reactionary declaration, reaching over 60 percent today. The U.S. Catholic Women's Ordination

Movement continues to organize for its cause and women's ordination groups have developed in other countries. Thus, the Vatican ban on women's ordination has become another area where official teachings are notably "not received" by the majority of Catholics.[7]

In June 2002 seven Catholic women were ordained by some Catholic bishops in Austria. Later several of these women priests were ordained bishops by these same bishops. They in turn have ordained more women priests. Thus an increasingly organized movement of Catholic women priests has formed who are developing formal rubrics for education and preparation for being ordained, first as deacons and then as priests. These women have often had decades of experience in parish ministry, chaplaincies, and retreat work. They are developing new ministries in such areas as universities, counseling, and local communities. By 2007 there were some forty women and a few men ordained in this movement and over 150 in preparation. The Vatican excommunicated the original seven ordained women in this movement and has refused to recognize it. But this movement is clearly filling a deep need among Catholic women, and it continues to grow.[8]

In November of 1976 the U.S. Catholic bishops organized the Call to Action, envisioned as a national synod of church renewal in Detroit. To their alarm, the delegates, assembled at the meeting to represent the laity, priests, and religious orders of each diocese, voted for various demands that the bishops found unacceptable: the ordination of women, the end to sexism in the church, married priests, and the acceptance of contraception and divorce. In May 1977, the National Conference of Catholic Bishops met in Chicago for their biannual meeting. Among their agenda items were the recommendations on women from the Detroit conference. Donna Quinn, Rosalie Muschal-Reinhardt, and Delores Brooks mobilized a number of other Catholic prowomen groups to come together to lobby the bishops on these issues. These groups rented a room in the Palmer House Hotel, where the bishops were meeting. Calling themselves the Women of the Church Coalition, they invited the bishops to dialogue with them on justice for women. Only two bishops, Raymond Lucker of New Ulm, Minnesota, and Charles Buswell of Pueblo, Colorado, responded to this invitation.[9]

In November of 1978 the Women's Ordination Conference held its second national conference in Baltimore, Maryland. This meeting was timed so that those women who wished to go to Washington for the bishops' meeting to lobby them on women's ordination could do so after the conference. As a result of this effort the bishops voted to enter into a formal dialogue with the Women's Ordination Conference. From 1979–82, the U.S. Catholic Bishops' Commission on Women met in official dialogue with the Women's Ordination Conference. This dialogue resulted in a recommendation for a full study on the question of women in the church. The U.S. Catholic bishops set up gatherings to listen to Catholic women's feelings about their roles in the church, using the data to write a pastoral letter on women. The WOC dialogue team strongly opposed the bishops' decision to write such a pastoral letter. Marjorie Tuite, one of the WOC team, suggested to the bishops that it would be better if women did a pastoral letter on bishops.

The first draft of the bishops' 1988 letter, "One in Christ: A Pastoral Response to the Concerns of Women for Church and Society," boldly asserted that "sexism is sin." The pastoral letter sought to ground male-female relations in family, society, and church in a model of "partnership." Men and women are created equally in the image of God and are to be partners in the family, partners in the work world, and partners in the ministry of the church. This approach revised traditional ideas of complementarity, which separated masculine and feminine "natures" and spheres into home and work. The bishops accepted that women are now a part of the work world, but upheld women's "vocation" as that of mother, while men were never said to have a "vocation" to be fathers. The pastoral letter also recommended an expansion of the lay ministries available to women in the church, as much as possible. Ordained ministry was still, however, off limits for discussion.

Pope John Paul II rejected the U.S. bishops' pastoral letter. The Vatican intervened during its drafting to insist on more explicit condemnations of birth control, abortion, and women's ordination. Moreover, the Pope replaced the language of partnership with his preferred term of "complementarity." Women had to be defined as having a "different" feminine nature that fits them for the domestic world. Women were not forbidden work and participation in public life, but these were seen as something forced upon them by inadequate social protection, not something due them as human beings. The U.S. bishops' pastoral went through several drafts in an effort to satisfy these papal demands and was finally tabled by the bishops in recognition of its unacceptability to U.S. Catholic women. By 1982 it appeared to women that this dialogue was unlikely to bear any real potential for change.

The insistence that women as women cannot be priests because maleness is necessary to the sacramental representation of Christ rests on a notion of an essential difference between women as "feminine" and men as "masculine." Most social thinkers today see such traditional separations of men and women as an outdated and disproven social bias that is inculcated by culture and education, and not a biological necessity.

CATHOLIC IDENTITY AND DIVERSE WOMEN

The more radical wing of Catholic feminism has come to question whether ordination itself is a desirable goal. They call for a dismantling of clerical hierarchies and for the organization of "women-church" worship communities. They believe that women who want ordination ought be granted it, but they argue that it would be unhealthy for a woman to put herself in this position in the present hierarchical system. The experience of ordained Protestant women is important in this regard. As more Protestant women are being ordained, they have found that such official ministry does not fully solve the problems of the inclusion and equality of women. Some ordained Protestant women have started women-church groups as support groups to nourish and sustain them alongside their participation in ordained ministry in the institutional church. The dialectic between inclusion of women in present structures and the need to nourish a more transformative vision of a nonsexist church continues, even after ordination has been won.

Some Catholic feminists suggested that ordination was not the primary goal for women. Rather the goal is organization of autonomous women's liturgical communities, or feminist base communities, where renewal of ministry in egalitarian participatory communities can take place directly. Some leaders of the loose coalition of groups that had come together as the Women of the Church Coalition decided to organize another major national conference, this time with the focus on building feminist communities, rather than on ordination. This conference, held in Chicago in November of 1983, drew over twenty-five hundred participants and set the pattern for subsequent women-church national conventions, with a combination of festive liturgies and intense workshops on a variety of feminist issues ranging from women's spirituality and justice for women in the church and society to questions of sexuality and reproductive rights.

Catholic identity obviously has a different meaning for groups that are women's offices of canonical orders than for groups with no ties to institutional Catholicism. But even while acknowledging a relation to a canonical order, the women leading these offices or networks express considerable doubt about their relation to the hierarchical male church. One nun said of her religious order:

Our religious identity is that of Roman Catholic women who are committed to a community that is also a papal institution. For some time we talked about pushing to become noncanonical, but now we do not think it is worth the effort. We see ourselves as proof that persons can be identified as Roman Catholic outside the structure of the parish.

But this same woman went on to express profound burn-out with efforts at church reform:

Also we are old. We have fought for the vernacular in the liturgy and we have been fired. We have fought not to wear the habit and we have had priests who said they respect us deride us. We have fought to keep schools open and have had parents call us money-grubbers. We fight to give our old sick sisters decent living and we are called middle-class. We fight for women's rights and we have women call us obsolete. Perhaps now our most significant struggle is to find a way to die well, with dignity and grace.[10]

A representative of the Loretto women's network responded to a question about religious identity—Catholic, ecumenical, or post-Christian—by saying:

I find this an intriguing question. We have never really discussed this as a network and I'm not sure how we'd respond to it. The Sisters of Loretto are, as you know, a canonical community of the Catholic

Church. At the same time, we have some co-members who are members of other faith communities, some who do not belong to any church and Sisters of Loretto who are totally disenchanted with the Roman Catholic hierarchical structure. . . . At the same time I know we see ourselves sufficiently rooted in Catholicism to choose to be in dialogue with the bishops (or one or two bishops) on any given subject—those that have to do especially with women, such as our God-given right and ability to make moral decisions; how some decisions of the hierarchy cannot stand because of their ignoring (not accepting) of this principle.

Perhaps what is most significant about the now more than twenty-year history of the American women-church movement is the extent to which most of its members are determined to remain with both sides of these ambiguities, without acceding to an either-or solution on one side or the other.

Generally women-church groups support the range of feminist issues in the church and in society. Most groups support reproductive rights, including legalized abortion and gay/lesbian rights in society. Some are involved particularly in antiracism work and issues of poverty of women and children. Antimilitarism and concern with U.S. intervention are broadly shared in principle. All would favor overcoming discrimination against women and gays in ordination and church employment, and making the church a democratic, participatory community, although there are differences on whether particular groups still want to give "energy" to church reform issues. Social justice is a concern of all women-church groups, although there has been division between academics concerned to have more intellectual analysis and those who want to focus on grassroots activism.

These shared social/moral principles do not make the activities of women-church groups tension-free, both within and among member groups. One important cause of conflict has been over racial-ethnic diversity. Although all groups would endorse the principle of more racial-ethnic inclusivity, and some are involved in community work across racial lines, how to make the Women-Church Convergence (WCC) itself more racially and ethnically diverse has been difficult. Subsequent national women-church conferences took place in Cincinnati in October of 1987 and in Albuquerque in April of 1993. The network of members of the Women-Church Convergence has continually expanded, with the addition of new local groups and women's offices of religious orders. Also the national conferences inspired the founding of new local groups. The national meetings continued to be festive events with growing attendance. However, power relations between different types of groups in different regions proved a problem. In addition, intense conflicts took place in the planning meetings of the Convergence over how best to promote greater racial and ethnic inclusivity.

For several years the National Assembly of Religious Women (NARW) came to Convergence meetings with the insistence that the national conferences be more racially and ethnically inclusive and give priority to empowering the leadership of women from black, Hispanic, Asian, Pacific Islander, and Native American backgrounds. In November of 1991 it issued an ultimatum to the members of the Women-Church Convergence that they make concerted efforts to make their meetings more racially/ethnically inclusive. In February 1992, NARW withdrew from the WCC. The Black Sisters Conference ceased to connect to the coalition early in the 1980s. Las Hermanas dropped out of the WCC in 1992 along with NARW and for the same reasons. As a consequence, WCC was more monocultural in 1996 than when its predecessor group began meeting in 1977.

WOMEN AND LITURGICAL LEADERSHIP

Although there is a range of women's identities along the spectrum of Catholic, ecumenical, and post-Christian, with some groups combining all three, most women-church groups have assumed the right and power to do their own liturgical celebrations "without benefit of clergy." The occasions for doing liturgy vary among groups. Some local groups get together for liturgy and mutual support as their primary activity. Others, particularly national groups, do not offer regular local liturgies but have a feminist liturgy as part of national conferences.

The pontificate of John Paul II made the ban on women's ordination, along with anticontraception and antiabortion, a touchstone of orthodoxy. The Pope claimed the Catholic Church could not change its teaching on this matter, and hence, open discussion of it was forbidden. Clergy who dis-

sented on this issue were not to be advanced to the episcopacy, which has meant an increasingly conservative Catholic
hierarchy. The current Pope Benedict XVI appears unlikely
to change this policy. The Vatican seeks to reassert control
over Catholic colleges and seminaries by demanding that
Catholic theologians receive a *mandatum* from the local
bishop. This includes acceptance of the ban on women's
ordination.

At the same time the Vatican has been holding back the
tide on women's ordination, the restriction of the priesthood
to celibate males has been awash in crises. Fewer men are
making themselves available for priesthood under such conditions, and some already ordained have opted out for marriage. As the numbers of Catholics continue to expand, the
church faces a crisis in its ability to provide priests for the
sacramental ministry of parishes. While the numbers of
priests in the United States has been in precipitous decline,
increasing numbers of Catholic women are earning decrees
in theological education and seeking ministries. Bishops are
turning by necessity to these theologically educated nuns
and laywomen for parish ministry and chaplaincies in pris-
ons, hospitals, and schools. Bishops are pressed to allow
women to administer parishes, preach, hear confessions, and
preside over Eucharistic celebrations.

The intransigence of the Pope and Vatican leaders and
the silencing and persecution of dissenters has made it unlikely that there will be any movement from the top on these
questions within the lifetime of Benedict XVI. Yet, as we
noted earlier in this essay, a lively movement that is ordaining

Catholic women priests has emerged since 2002. Will official Catholicism eventually recognize them and accept the legitimacy of their orders? Or will it continue to shun them, but eventually accept a more docile group of women as priests?

Historical experience has shown that what the Catholic Church has to do for its own survival it is likely to do eventually. Like John XXIII's turnabout on liberalism, a future Pope is likely to seek ways to ease the impasse between Catholic women, who assume self-determination in sexual and social life, and the church's need for women to continue as the mainstay of church membership and, increasingly, of pastoral ministry.

History shows that reform in the Catholic Church seldom comes from the Vatican, but from the real world experiences of Catholics who dissent from the dogmatic stances of the hierarchy until it is required to change. There has been an increasing recognition that the oppression of women is not God's will, but is unjust and sinful. Although the present Pope continues to conduct a reactionary backlash against feminism, most Catholics have come to accept women's equality in society and in the church and see little reason why women cannot be ordained. There is also widespread dissent against traditional teachings on sexuality and reproduction. Although the Vatican may try to hold the line on acceptance of progressive views, it is unlikely that it will convince the majority of Catholics. Whether it moves soon or in the distant future remains to be seen. Hopefully, it is only a matter of time before church teaching adapts itself to deeper visions of liberation in Christianity and progressive Catholicism.

5

A Discipleship of Equals

From the beginning, the Christian church saw itself as a community of liberation from slavery and oppression. It drew on the ancient theme of Israel as a community in exodus from slavery in Egypt on a journey to the Promised Land. Baptism, the ritual of conversion and transformation for entering the Christian community, delivered Christians into the Christ-nature. That nature overcame all social hierarchies of ethnicity, class, and gender in the community. There was to be no discrimination between Jew or Greek, slave or free, male or female. Church leaders soon, however, spiritualized this discipleship of equals and denied the clear, concrete references to changing real social hierarchies.

They reinstated a patriarchal system in the New Testament household codes. Wives were told to obey their husbands, children their parents, and slaves their masters. The codes reiterated a demand for subordinates to obey their lords. These injunctions give us strong evidence that many Christians understood baptism and entry into the church as overcoming these relationships of domination socially, as well as spiritually. Obviously, there is no reason to create strong prohibitions against something unless it is occurring.

Christian history shows how the vision of the church as a community of liberation has been continually rediscovered. The priesthood of all believers with all sharing ministry is found, for example, in medieval Beguine communities, in Quaker meetings, and Methodist Sunday schools. The vision is alive and well around the world today in Christian communities in the United States and in Asia, Africa, and Latin America. Although the critique of patriarchy has been implicit in these reclamations of face-to-face, communitarian churches, this critique has seldom been made explicit. Thus the current development of women-church and feminist forms of community represent a major new step toward dismantling the patriarchal and sinful distortion of human existence. They offer church as a community of liberation from patriarchy and its hierarchies. If the church is a community of liberation from patriarchy, then it should most particularly witness to an alternative pattern of relationship between its members.

Patriarchy is not the world order God created. It is a historically constructed system in which ruling-class males have established themselves in a position of domination over women and over dependent classes, such as slaves, children, and racial or ethnic groups. They deem such dependent others as inferior. Ruling-class males have built social structures and ideologies of justification for these social structures to monopolize cultural, economic, and political power in society. Other people have been forbidden access to this power and confined to auxiliary status as physical laborers in production and reproduction, while ruling-class males own, command, and consume the lion's share of the fruits of this labor. Rejecting patriarchy in society also means rejecting it as the appropriate order for the church.

The order of relationships for the church should be a discipleship of equals and mutual empowerment. It should witness to this just relationship of humans to each other and to the rest of creation by embodying alternative relations in its ministry, sacraments, educational work, administration, and mission to society. A church which embodies the worst patterns of oppression, while claiming to offer liberation, is simply unbelievable.

CREATING A LIBERATING CHURCH

Constructing a Catholic Church of liberation from patriarchy requires dismantling clericalism. Clericalism is utterly incompatible with a liberative understanding of church and ministry. It separates ministry from mutual empowerment in community and creates castes of clergy over laity in a hierarchical order. Ministry becomes the special preserve of the ordained, rather than being the work of an entire community that is articulated within and by it. The clergy monopolize sacramental action, education, administration, and leadership in mission. Clericalism turns the laity into passive dependents who receive these services from the clergy and carry out their orders, but they do not participate in shaping and defining the activities they are asked to carry out.

In the official Catholic myth of origins, Christ himself, God's representative, established the ordained episcopacy to

carry on his presence in the world. Christ founded the hierarchy to pass down his divine power through a line of succession, beginning with the apostle Peter. Bishops in this line of
succession dispense this power to priests through ordination,
and priests in turn dispense forgiveness and access to the
grace of God to the laity. But the laity must submit to the
rules laid down by the hierarchy. In this way the entire sacramental and educational life of the church is distorted into a
power tool of the clergy over the laity, as well as a hierarchy of
clergy, with bishops over priests, archbishops over bishops,
and Pope over bishops.

Clericalism is built on and duplicates patriarchy. The
basic symbol and mode of the clerical relation is that of the
all-knowing and all-powerful husband over a passive, dependent wife, combined with the all-powerful and all-knowing
father over dependent, undeveloped children. Instead of the
father-husband cleric helping the children-wife-layperson to
develop and become equals, the basic mode of ministry
reenforces dependency, ignorance, and arrested development. Patriarchy in the church disempowers the people
sacramentally, educationally, and politically.

In sacramental life—life grounded in the divine and experienced communally—the clergy alienate the people by
using rituals and symbols as magical tools of control. The key
to an alienated sacramental life is the divorce of grace from
nature and of redemption from creation. The patriarchal
church defines grace as something transcendent that negates
nature as evil or inferior. Power to deliver grace rests in the
hierarchically ordered representatives of an institution that

claims it alone mediates this supernatural power. For example, clericalism turns baptism into a rite by which one rejects one's natural life, derived from birth, and undergoes a rebirth that overcomes and transcends the sinful, mortal life one received from one's parents due to their sinful sex.

The Eucharist should be a symbol of our participation in authentic life, our nurture and growth in such life. Clericalism has turned it into the symbol most radically alienated from the people. The Eucharist was transformed into a tool of clerical power over the people and is the sacrament most rigidly guarded as a clerical privilege, a sacred act that no lay person can perform. Ordination is the hierarchically transmitted power to "confect" the Eucharist. Until Vatican II, priests mumbled the ritual in Latin, a language most people could not understand. Now, the current Pope, Benedict XVI, has opened doors to the return to the "mystery" of the Latin, with the restoration of the Trentine Counter-Reformation rite of the Mass. Thus the simple act of blessing and distributing food and drink as a symbol of giving and nurturing life is turned into a power tool to control access to God and a redeeming relation to God and the community of Christ. Excommunication, or denial of the Eucharist, is the prime tool used to punish those who resist clerical control.

Disempowering education is a second aspect of clericalism. The clergy have historically monopolized theological education, making it inaccessible to the people. Theological education was developed in a language unknown to the people, either in ecclesiastical Latin, which neither laity nor nuns were taught, or else in a learned jargon that most people do not understand. The people are thus made to feel helpless and dependent on the clergy for interpretation of scripture and analysis of theological symbols and ideas. In addition, for many centuries, the church withheld the reading of the scriptures themselves from laypeople. Although Protestantism represented a reappropriation of Bible reading by the laity, it also soon developed esoteric methods of biblical interpretation that lay people felt incompetent to rival and that required preachers to explain. Thus, we see a common pattern in church renewal movements by which egalitarian movements are reclericalized as the movement becomes institutionalized.

Today, the increased education of the laity means that many Catholic lay people now have a more modern and sophisticated knowledge of theology, church, history, and the Bible than most traditionally educated priests and bishops. This widespread education threatens clericalism. A great number of lay people now have some theological education, either from college religion courses or from seminaries with lay education programs; some have earned doctorates in theological subjects. Liberation theology and their base communities in Latin American reinstituted lay Bible reading. Bishops and the Vatican have tried to forbid qualified laity, especially women, from teaching in Catholic seminaries that train priests, going so far as to prohibit women from attending Catholic seminaries.

In Catholicism, the most hierarchical of all Christian churches, the laity traditionally have had no role in church administration. Lay people could neither participate in calling pastors to their churches nor in ordaining them. They were not elected to church councils at a diocesan level, much less at national or international levels. They could not write or vote on laws governing the church. The Second Vatican Council tried to change the stratified pattern of church government into a more collegial relation of Pope with bishops, bishops with priests, and priests with laity. But the Vatican quickly rejected real power sharing. Minimal progress in allowing lay ministry in parishes and the participation of laity in church councils became necessary partly due to extreme shortages of clergy. The priest, however, holds the final decision-making power about policy and can ignore the advice of the laity and dismiss the church council at will. Hence, the whole system remains despotic, despite some priests who wish to be more collaborative in leadership. There is no final accountability to the people and no true democracy.

Clericalism is the expropriation of sacramental life, theological education, and church administration from the people. A ministry of the discipleship of equals is, therefore, a revolutionary process of reappropriating to the people what has been falsely taken from us. We are reclaiming sacramental life as our rightful entry into redemptive life. Our mutual empowerment in authentic human life is freed from alienating power. We understand theological education and teaching as our own reflections on the meaning of reclaiming our authentic life from such distortion. Ministry is the active work and reflection upon that life; it is also the building of redemptive communities as the bases from which to challenge systems and ideologies of oppression and injustice.

A discipleship of equals understands ministry as function, rather than as clerical caste. Lumping all ministry into an ordained caste means that many of the community's needs go unmet, since no one person possesses all these skills and gifts. A discipleship of equals delegates various tasks to people who have the skills and readiness to undertake these tasks. The dismantling of clerical concepts of ministry and church organization does not require rejecting any leadership roles and skills. However, we must insist the community itself decides what expressions of liturgy, learning, and service it needs to express its redemptive life.

Baptism is the proclamation of our entrance into a process of *metanoia*, or turning around. It enables us to see through the justifications for oppressive systems and get in touch with our true potential for life together. Eucharist is the ongoing nurture of life in community. These rites need to be rewritten to bring out these meanings.

A ministry of function can allow the many ministerial needs of the community to be defined and met. It can draw on the skills and gifts of a variety of people in the community and thus activate their gifts in ministry. Redemptive, creative church communities need a variety of enablers needs: 1) liturgical creators, poets, artists, choreographers, dramatists, and preachers; 2) teachers who know the history of religious ideologies and their relationship to various social systems and who can help the community reflect on and reconstruct its inherited symbols; 3) administrators skilled in organizing and developing the material resources of the

community; 4) community organizers who can critically analyze the structures of social oppression and organize the
community for social change; and 5) spiritual counselors who
have deep wisdom about the inner life and can be guides to
others in the journey of life. Such roles should not create a
permanent caste of leaders set aside for life. Instead, the
community should determine functional roles for leaders
based on its needs. I suspect most communities will need
someone to coordinate these many processes and oversee
them all, but that person must remain truly a *primus inter
pares*, first among equals, rather than a hierarch.

The leaders of the church should always be engaged in
reproducing themselves, educating others so they can also
fulfill these roles for the community. Participating with
someone who is skilled in creating and leading liturgy should
be a process of learning the same skills. Helping in community organizing with a skilled organizer should produce people who can take the lead in the same process. Being in
spiritual counseling should produce people who can guide
others. Instead of an education for permanent dependency,
education should empower and make the educated into
peers of the educator.

A DISCIPLESHIP OF EQUALS

Many of the communities I have known, both Catholic and
ecumenical, have demonstrated that living out a vision of a
discipleship of equals is not only possible, but life giving and

liberating. Each has had its own character and value, as each has sought to live out just and mutually enhancing relationships, even as it worked for a better world.

For almost forty years, I have been a member of the board of Catholics for a Free Choice and its Latin American sister group, Catolicas por el Derecho de Decidir. Among our many functions is to develop and offer Catholics clear ethical guidelines to defend a more just sexual ethics. We usually combine our meetings with other activities, with conferences of our Latin American colleagues, either in Washington or in a Latin American venue, or with protest marches in Washington on both the U.S. government and the Vatican Embassy. We have met at the New York assembly of the UN itself, as right-wing groups, especially the Vatican, seek to undermine its work for women's reproductive health. We have traveled to UN conferences around the world. Our board meetings are truly a gathering of good friends.

Another Catholic group that has been important to me is Call to Action (CTA). It began in Chicago when the U.S. Catholic bishops organized the first Call to Action meeting at the time of the U.S. bicentennial in 1976. When Cardinal Cody of Chicago declined to organize a delegation, a group of Chicago Catholics organized on our own. The national gathering quickly overran the bishops' desires, so they shut it down. However, since the Chicago group was not under the bishops' control, we continued to meet and grew into a national group, with a huge yearly meeting, as well as regional meetings. For many Catholics, CTA is a lifeline to a true vision of an alternative, more liberative vision of the church.

The network continues to grow. I have spoken at national CTA meetings almost every year for more than thirty years and look forward to it as a way of networking with a community of progressive U.S. Catholics, one that increasingly draws on the global progressive Catholic community.

The Con-spirando community in Latin America publishes *Con-spirando*, a journal of feminist theology and eco-feminism, founded in 1992. Composed mostly of Catholic feminist groups of Latin Americans based in Santiago, Chile, Con-spirando brings together a network of writers, artists, liturgists, and therapists across Latin America. They have embarked on many creative research projects. One such initiative organized eleven teams in different Latin American countries that researched the legends and liturgical practices in festivals devoted to Mary. Each team sought not only to assess how these sites preserved pre-Hispanic goddesses or female divinities and female-centered religiosity, but also how these practices might help in the development of a feminist spirituality for Latin American women today. The result is the 2004 book *Virgenes y Diosas en American latina: La resignification de lo sagrado (Virgins and Goddesses in Latin America: The Resignification of the Sacred)*.

The Women's Commission of the Ecumenical Association of Third World Theologians (EATWOT) brings together Christian feminist theologians from Latin America, Africa, and Asia, as well as U.S. minority women. They develop their reflections in their own contexts and share them through networks, joint projects, and publications, such as their journal *Voices*. The African group, which named themselves the

"Circle of Concerned African Women Theologians," has developed a project to reflect theologically on AIDS in Africa. They are seeking to overcome the fear of AIDS and are helping Africans to take hold of this terrible pandemic devastating their societies. Although I am not eligible to be a member of the EATWOT Women's Commission, I have been privileged to be in dialogue with its development since its beginning in Geneva, Switzerland, in 1982 and have spoken at some of its meetings.

Schools of theological education where I have taught have been essential to my life as communities of colleagues where I shared many aspects of my life. I was at Garrett-Evangelical Theological Seminary in Evanston, Illinois, for twenty-seven years, and there my colleagues and I created and maintained a covenanted community of mutual support and liturgy for twenty years. Also, several of the theological Schools in the Chicago area worked with the Center for Alternative Technology to create the Interreligious Sustainability Project of Greater Chicago. This coalition spent two years discussing the design for an urban ecology project that would draw on many religious congregations, Christian, Jewish, Muslim, Ba'hai, and others. We saw such congregations as key bases for neighborhood organizing for ecological sustainability. The group proposed a variety of ideas and community organizations for alternative ways of living in the city as a total bioregion. In our second stage of community organizing, we went through the congregations to reach out to neighborhoods. Neighborhood activities were always undertaken with a sense of relating these to each other and to the whole greater Chicago bioregion. This was a model project of how religious congregations can work together with neighborhoods and cities to create more livable cities.

The ministry of theological education is to enable students to become fellow teacher-scholars. After retiring from Garrett, I was on the faculty of the Graduate Theological Union (GTU) in Berkeley, California, from 2000–2005. I now teach at the Claremont School of Theology and School of Religion of the Claremont Graduate University. In all these schools, my students have been as much a part of my community as my faculty colleagues. I regard my students, preparing for ministry or for teaching, as friends who are in the process of becoming peers and colleagues, and I have delighted to continue my friendship with them as my former students entered ministry or teaching positions.

These days, I experience liberation community at Pilgrim Place, a retirement community for church workers and religious educators, which my husband and I joined in 2002. Everyone in this community of three hundred and fifty has come from a background in church service, education, or ministry, from around the world as well as in the United States. Seven members of the Garrett faculty are now resident in this community, as well as some members of the Claremont faculties. Several faculty members from the GTU will also come here upon retiring. We have chosen to grow old together in this Christian community, which includes Catholics and people from many different Protestant traditions. Strongly committed to justice and peace, members of the community conduct a silent witness against war every Friday afternoon near the interstate highway.

Peace and justice groups at Pilgrim Place constantly offer lectures and discussion on different social issues, as well as opportunities for involvement in organizations working for change. Many volunteer to help homeless, poor, or marginalized people. Members are constantly finding new steps for better sustainability. Recently, grass was removed around the main buildings to be replanted with drought-resistant California native plants. The community maintains two gardens, as well as over a hundred fruit trees, scattered throughout the "campus" from which a weekly farmers market is offered to the community. The proceeds go to a fund for those residents in need of help with medical expenses. This fund also helps equalize the residence expenses of those with more limited economic assets.

Although there is no official denominational identity, there is a liturgical life here. The vespers every Thursday take many different forms and are led by volunteers. Pilgrim Place has also decided to become a eucharistic community—twice a month volunteers design and lead an ecumenical Eucharist. Our women-church group also offers a feminist Eucharist service once a month, which draws participants from the larger Los Angeles community, but more than half of those who attend come from our community. This community in Claremont also has many other active women's groups, which read books together and organize around peace and justice issues.

Pilgrim Place's residents, ranging in age from sixty to over one hundred years of age, help one another through what the Latin Americans call *la tercer edad*, the third age of life. In addition to a host of social, cultural, and sporting activities, the community supports a nursing facility that cares for the sick and dying, and many take turns as chaplains. When people are dying, their friends gather around to guide them through a process according to the ways they have specified as how they wish to die, and almost everyone is present for funerals, usually planned ahead with input from the deceased. These memorials punctuate the life of the community every few weeks, a frequent occurrence in a group of people at this stage of life, though the community is remarkably good at keeping people healthy and creative well into our third age.

These many expressions of community are engaged in the work of liberation at local, national, and global levels. They are what keep me alive and continually restore my faith that "Another world is possible," the slogan of the World Social Forum that meets yearly in Porto Alegre, Brazil. We do not have to acquiesce to oppressive and violent relationships, as if they were an unchangeable order of things for the church, for American society, or for the world. Against all odds, we can continue to stand up for an alternative, more life-giving, more redemptive way of being in relationship to one another as people of love and justice, as people who care for the earth and creation, as people who remember the vision of our brother Jesus who preached good news to the poor, the liberation of the captives, and the setting at liberty of those who are oppressed—truly, a discipleship of equals.

6

Liberation for the Poor
and Oppressed

In the 1950s the nations of Central and South America had
been struggling, especially since World War II, with a
many-factored crisis. Neocolonial industrialization had
widened the gap between rich and poor; unemployment
grew in festering urban slums, aggravated by expanding pop-
ulations; inflation burgeoned; and staggering national debt
kept escalating. The official international answer to these
trends was "development." Western Europe and the United
States would provide aid through public and private sources
to help "underdeveloped" countries achieve the build-up of
capital for industrialization. The assumption behind this approach was that the countries of the "Third," formerly colonized worlds of Latin America, Asia, and Africa could be
judged by how far along the road they were moving toward
realizing the same model that had been followed by western
"developed" nations.

In the 1960s, some Latin American economists began to
dissent from this model. They argued that Latin America was
not suffering from "underdevelopment," but from misdevel-

opment. Latin Americans had not been slumbering for four centuries while Yankees were hard at work pulling themselves up by their bootstraps. Rather, Latin American poverty was the underside of wealthy industrialized countries building up their capital base through the extraction of resources from colonized regions by slave and serf labor. With the European colonization of Central and South America in the sixteenth century, there began a history of relationships that fed the wealth of the industrialized regions at the expense of colonized regions through exploitation and dependency. Latin America is poor because it was and is so rich; rich in metals, minerals, temperate climates, and fertile land. Colonizing powers used this wealth to finance the industrialization of Europe and North America, leaving Central and Latin America and the Caribbean stripped and depleted. This pattern continues in new stages to the present.[1]

To these critical economists of the 1960s and 1970s, it became apparent that more "development" coming from these same colonizing centers of power only increased the structural dependency of Latin America and the impoverishment of the majority of its people. Western industrialization was not concerned with meeting the needs of the masses of Latin American people. Rather it continued to use the cheap resources and labor of Latin America to make money for the wealthy of the North. Sociologists and economists critical of this pattern of dependent "development" began to speak of "liberation."

CHRISTIAN THEOLOGY FOR LIBERATION

Latin American liberation theology emerged in the mid-1960s in response to this neocolonial crisis of poverty and political oppression. It advocated revolutionary changes in the political dependency of Latin American nations on the elites of the North. Liberation meant nationalizing the ownership of the resources of Latin America, taking them from foreign ownership or control. It meant creating a new plan of integral development to meet the needs of Latin Americans, starting with their basic need for affordable food and housing, health services and education, and better-paid jobs. This would be a development from the bottom up, not a colonizing development to enrich the North and a small Latin American elite. Liberation theologians and theorists assumed that a form of democratic socialism, not American- or European-style capitalism, was needed to make this liberating change.

In the 1960s a model for this alternative development was Cuba. Cuba, many felt, was moving down the path of decolonization and socialism that other Latin American peoples should follow. Che Guevara embodied the romantic type of guerrilla fighter who would carry the Cuban revolution to other Latin American countries. Camilo Torres, the martyred guerrilla priest of Colombia, joined Che as a symbol of revolution. Many activists called Christians to join Marxists in the struggle for liberation. When I visited Bogota in 1970 it was common to see cars sporting the silhouettes of Che and Camilo as new heroes or new Christs.

The U.S. response to these events was the Kennedy administration's Alliance for Progress. It sought to show that capitalist development could solve the problems of poverty better than Cuban socialism. This goal, however, included efforts to invade Cuba and overthrow its new government, or, failing that, to choke it to death economically through an international embargo. The more idealistic plans of the Alliance for Progress were pushed aside for a focus on counterinsurgent military aid. Police and military hardware and training in their use, including torture, shaped new military forces in Latin America whose purpose was primarily the repression of internal dissent.

Beginning in 1964 with the coup in Brazil, a new kind of military regime emerged in Latin America that spread from the mid-1960s to the 1980s. These "national security states" might be described as a kind of colonial fascism, dependent on foreign aid from neocolonial centers of power in the North. Such states acted as conduits for economic exploitation on behalf of the interests of these outside powers. Latin American national security states in Brazil, Argentina, Chile, Paraguay, Uruguay, and Bolivia dismantled the institutions of civil society. They repressed opposition parties, labor unions, student organizations, peasant unions, open universities, and a free press and subjugated them to military juntas ruling through the army and secret police. Many of the leaders of these states were graduates of the U.S.-sponsored School of the Americas and dependent on U.S. funding. The ideologies of these totalitarian states focused on prevention of "communist subversion," and they often saw themselves as defending "Christian civilization."

As the new military juntas destroyed opposition and created terrorist regimes, with secret police, torture chambers, hidden camps of political prisoners, and hit lists of enemies, the Catholic Church played an important new role. It became the surrogate for civil society. As the only autonomous institution left, the church was the only place where some protest could be mounted, where people could meet, and some semblance of independent communication maintained. Even if the government periodically jammed church-funded radio stations, handbills could be tacked to church doors.

Bishops, such as Helder Camera of Brazil or Oscar Romero of El Salvador, preached critical sermons, which were passed hand to hand or eagerly listened to on the radio. Committees of solidarity, such as the one formed in Chile after the U.S.-sponsored coup in 1973, both fed the poor and protested disappearances of activists and civil rights violations. Bishops who were moderates became radicalized when their priests and religious and lay catechists were tortured and killed. In 1976 an entire gathering of bishops in Riobamba, Ecuador, was arrested and imprisoned for three days. Thousands of nuns and priests were among tens of thousands of disappeared persons or among those whose bodies showed up with torture marks to terrorize the population. A church making even small gestures of solidarity with the poor found it quickly lost any invulnerability it imagined it enjoyed and became a church of martyrs.

In the mid-1960s some theologians, such as Gustavo Gutierrez of Peru, formulated a liberation theology, rooted in the prophetic tradition of the Bible and in contemporary social analysis.[2] This new theology was communicated through progressive networks of pastoral leaders throughout Latin America. In 1968 the newly organized Latin American Bishops' Conference (CELAM) met for its first major gathering in Medellín, Colombia (after an initial organizational meeting in 1955). The attendance of bishops was small and there was little popular consultation in advance. The theologian advisers were heavily weighted toward those who were emerging as the theologians of liberation, including Gutierrez. Helder Camera of Brazil was the leading influence among the bishops. The document that emerged committed the church to the cause of the poor, condemned the "international imperialism of money," named violence first of all as the institutionalized violence of poverty and state repression, and pledged the church to build a new economic order freed from dependency.

These themes gave legitimacy to the liberation perspective through the blessings of the Latin American hierarchy. These views were quickly carried into the radical practices of young priests and pastoral leaders, such as the Golconda movement in Colombia and Christians for Socialism in Chile. Some bishops were astonished by the document of Medellín signed in their name. Even though it was an official statement of CELAM, many traditional Catholics saw it as the work of a radical leftist group. These more conservative leaders began to organize to take the leadership of CELAM out of the hands of the liberationists.

In 1972 Monsignor Lopez Trujillo of Bogota, Colombia,

was elected secretary for CELAM and began organizing the conservatives for the next CELAM meeting to reverse the work of Medellín. At the 1979 meeting in Puebla, Mexico, CELAM organizers excluded liberation theologians from preparing the document for Puebla and from serving as delegates or advisors. Nonetheless, a large number of liberation theologians attended auxiliary sessions organized outside of the official gathering. A feminist group, Women for Dialogue, also held concurrent meetings. Progressive ideas found their way into the official meeting, and the final document reaffirmed most of the commitments of Medellín, but it had a broader consensus.

The Vatican under the pontificate of John Paul II and the leadership of the head of the Holy Office for the Doctrine of the Faith, Cardinal Ratzinger, disapproved of and warned against liberation theology.[3] John Paul II consistently appointed conservative bishops to replace progressive ones. For example, to succeed Helder Camera in Recife, Brazil, the Pope appointed a highly conservative bishop who closed down the seminary that prepared priests using a method of immersion in the lives of the poor. The progressive faculty, including ecofeminist Ivone Gebara, lost their positions as teachers and were scattered. The Vatican also imposed prohibitions on leading liberation theologians, such as Leonardo Boff. He opted to resign from the priesthood and become a lay theologian.[4]

Throughout these events, liberation theology consolidated and matured, culminating in the magisterial collection of the major thinkers of liberation theology, *Mysterium Lib-*

erationis: Conceptos fundamentales de la Teología de Liberación, edited by Jon Sobrino and Ignacio Ellacuría in El Salvador, which appeared in 1991, delayed by Ellacuría's assassination in 1989. This collection represents the classic period of liberation theology, both its power in the face of government oppression and its limitations. Although four women appear in its pages, they are confined to the "feminine" topics of "Women and the Theology of Liberation" and "Mary." Absent are the voices of African-Latinos and indigenous people, a more explicit feminist theology, and concern for the environment. Protestants, although a part of liberation theology from the 1960s, were not asked to contribute.[5]

Latin American liberation theology saw crises and transition between 1989 and 1991. Some of the major writers were dead or marginalized from the church. The disintegration of the Soviet Union and the rise of the United States as the world's sole superpower, with its neoliberal hegemonic economic system, seemed to indicate the end of revolutionary options throughout the world. Liberation theology was declared "dead." North American and European theological schools generally ceased to read Latin American theology, and there was a great decrease in its translation into English.

The announcement of liberation theology's demise was both parochial and premature.[6] With violence, poverty, and oppression worsening in the world, a whole new generation of Latin American theologians, from indigenous, Afro-Latin, and feminist perspectives, emerged. Thus, we should speak of liberation theology's different stages, one from 1968–90, and a second stage from 1900 to today. Ignacio Ellacuría was the culmination and most profound exponent of the "classic" stage of liberation theology, and Ivone Gebara, the most creative Latin American theologian writing from an ecofeminist perspective, is an example of its current flowering.

IGNACIO ELLACURÍA

Ellacuría was born in Bilbao, Spain, on November 9, 1930, entered the Jesuit novitiate in 1947, and went to El Salvador in 1949, studying there and in Ecuador before becoming a Salvadoran citizen. From 1962 he studied philosophy with the Spanish philosopher Xavier Zubiri and became his close friend and collaborator. In El Salvador, Ellacuría led the drive to commit Jesuits to the promotion of justice as the defining characteristic of their mission. Appointed rector of the Jesuit-founded Central American University in 1979, he shaped the university to promote liberating transformation of the national society. Under threats from the right-wing government, Ellacuría left El Salvador several times, but returned repeatedly to continue negotiating a settlement to the civil war that raged in the country, a war heavily funded by the United States.

Ellacuría was critical of the Western intellectual traditions of idealism that separated intellect from sensation, turning knowledge into abstract logic and viewing reality as static "objects." For Ellacuría sensation and intellect are united in one faculty, the sentient intellect. The human person always both experiences reality through sensation and at the same time recognizes this reality as independent of the self. This concept of the sentient intellect overcomes the problems of Western epistemology that seeks to bridge the false gap between intellectual "ideas" and sensory reality. Humans possess options for choice, the basis of freedom. Their choices interact with reality and reshape it; these re-shaped realities become the historical context for new human choices. Thus sentient intellect is always historically located and is the result of past human praxis (action/thinking shaping reality) that has already shaped reality and becomes the context for new praxis.

Human choices are not random, but have a purposive di-rection, to improve human chances for survival. Since hu-mans depend for their survival on the world, actions to improve survival always happen in communities. Through a trajectory of praxis expanding to meet physical needs and personal liberation, more human capacities are liberated. Physical and biological needs are not left behind but are in-corporated into cultural forces. Human praxis thus becomes the driving force of transformed reality toward enhanced freedom for a widening community.

Ellacuría concluded that human historical praxis aims ul-timately at the liberation of all humanity. The oppressed, marginalized, and impoverished play a key role in "signs of the times," indicating humanity's current stage in this progress toward human liberation. They are the leading edge and indicators of history's progress toward the greater hu-manization of reality, and they save the privileged from a false life of self-enrichment at the expense of others. The privileged, whose needs are met and who have wider areas of freedom, are obligated to work for the impoverished, who lack the basic necessities for human liberation. Together, all create a society where more and more people are freed from basic wants and can become more fully human.[7]

Ellacuría's historical understanding of reality defines the Christian faith historically. He argued that Christian faith was distorted through Platonic idealism, which dehistorized Jesus Christ, the cross, the resurrection, sin, and salvation. Ellacuría urged Christian faith to recover its historicity, its meaning both in history and as history.[8] The critical question for understanding Jesus' life, death, and resurrection is not "why did he die, but *why did they kill him.*" The question "why did he die," takes Jesus' death as a Platonic, abstract transaction between God and the sinful human being outside any historical context. The human being, defined as sinful or alienated from God, is given a generic ahistorical state of "fallenness," who can then be restored eternally to God through Jesus' death, which "pays for our sins." The question of why Jesus died is answered without historical context or content: "He died to save us from our sins."

Ellacuría's question, "why did they kill him," propels us into a different understanding of Jesus' death in its historical context. Historical actors executed him: the Roman governor of Palestine, with the collaboration of Jewish religious leaders under Roman occupation. Why did they kill him? Because Jesus lived in a certain way, as a prophetic denouncer of those who oppressed the poor and marginalized; he announced the good news of liberation to these oppressed people. His denunciation of injustice and annunciation of good

news threatened the security of those in control. As benefici-
aries of Roman power, they enjoyed wealth and ease at the
expense of others, and they executed him in a particular way.
They hung him on a cross to die a very public and excruciat-
ing death. Thus, they sought to terrorize and silence those
who might wish to continue his liberating praxis. Only when
Christians rediscover the historical context of Jesus' life do
we realize the meaning of his death on the cross.[9]

The crucified Christ did not simply die (as all finite beings die) but was executed by those who refused his message.
Jesus did not come to "suffer and die," as though suffering
and dying were the purpose of his life. His mission was to
proclaim that God "has anointed me to bring good news to
the poor" (Luke 4:18). Good news to the poor meant that
their unjust oppression was to be overcome. The system that
both impoverishes the many and enriches the few must be
changed; a new relation must be established that gives to all
their basic necessities and works to humanize all people.[10]

The impoverished and oppressed today are the continu-
ation of the Crucifixion. The historical meaning of their misery is rooted in the same forces of evil that crucified Christ
and continue to crucify the poor today. The crucified poor
are the "Servants of God," who testify to God's liberating
message, for which the powerful crucified Christ. God in
Christ continues to call us to repent and to join in solidarity
with the poor to complete the liberation of humanity.[11]

Those who make "a preferential option for the poor"
must not idealize poverty, but end this suffering, take the
crucified down from the cross, and create a new human soci-

ety where there is no more oppressor or oppressed. Salvation means real decisions by real people to "repent" of unjust power or to transform passive acceptance of injustice for real struggle to overcome evil. This repentance has both personal and structural aspects. Personally, it means choices to commit one's own life to justice against unjust social realities. Structurally, it means real practices to change systems that impoverish some to enrich others, and to create new social relations that more justly give the means of life to all. Ellacuría insists that it does no good to envision and announce a distant paradise, while doing nothing to improve life for the poor today. The Kingdom of God is both a symbol for the completion of all hopes and a demand for practical steps for realizing real hopes today.

The opposite of the Kingdom of God is the Kingdom of Sin. A system of legal, social, and economic patterns, it gives unjust wealth and power to the few by impoverishing the many. This system has ideologies that justify this injustice (by, for example, claiming that the poor are lazy or are racially inferior and thus incapable of intelligent action). It continually reproduces unjust patterns by conditioning people to accept them as normal, natural, and the will of God. The false ideal of human life promoted by capitalist affluence of the rich at the expense of the majority is individualism, lack of solidarity with others, ethnocentrism and racism, the idolatry of the nation-state, and the exploitation of others. It mobilizes various forms of violent power to repress dissent. This was Ellacuría's El Salvador in which the rich used the military to torture and murder all who questioned their power. It too was both personal and structural. The Kingdom of Sin was perpetuated not only by socialization and political systems but also by the oppressors' personal decisions to ally themselves with and to defend a violent and unjust system. Ellacuría faced concretely the troubling reality that for much of its history, particularly as auxiliaries to the colonization of Latin America by the Spanish in the sixteenth century, the Roman Catholic Church was a tool of oppression, not of liberation.[12]

The mission of the church is to convert humanity from this "old man" of capitalist sinfulness. The church of Christ, for Ellacuría, is the community that carries the memory of the crucified Christ and that opts for the Kingdom of God by aligning itself with the crucified poor. That community of the followers of Christ continues in history his mission of announcing good news to the poor, the liberation of the captives, and denunciation of the forces of injustice that perpetuate misery and oppression. That community takes up the risks of the cross; it risks the counterattack of those who seek to silence the prophets and to maintain the unjust system. The church of Christ acts to denounce injustice and to encourage repentance and transformation in concrete situations. It stands in solidarity with the poor and awakens them to struggle for the creation of a more just society. The truth of the church is judged, not by its theoretical discourse, but by its actions that shape history toward liberation. It is only through such actions that it can be said to be the "sacrament of salvation," where liberating action is happening. The church is not the only place where such action is happening, but it is the place that is aware of the theological implications of liberating action and promotes such actions as its central mission.[13]

From 1976–1990 a state of civil war tormented El Salvador in which tens of thousands died. Among these were leading priests, nuns, and church leaders. In 1977, the government assassinated a priest, Rutilio Grande, who worked with the poor. The murder transformed the newly elected archbishop of San Salvador, Oscar Romero, friend to both Grande and Ellacuría. Romero, previously a conservative, became a prophetic and outspoken voice for justice. He, too, was assassinated in 1980 as he celebrated Mass. On November 16, 1989, in the early hours of the morning, the government's Atlacatl battalion went to the Jesuit residence at the university where they assassinated Ellacuría and five other resident Jesuits, and their housekeeper and her daughter. The murders shocked the world and forced the United States to withdraw some aid and to press for token punishment of the assassins. Peace accords ending the civil war were finally signed in January 1992.[14]

North American news media continued to claim after his death that Ellacuría supported armed violence,[15] and, of course, the El Salvadorian elite did so too. That the United States was the chief funder of such state violence makes such critique especially hypocritical. The critique falsifies Ellacuría's position on armed violence. It also reflects the assumption that violence is fine when used to support the dominant powers but bad when opposition forces seek to change an unjust system. Ellacuría, like other liberation theologians, saw armed violence on behalf of changing a violent, unjust system as the recourse of last resort. In this they simply followed traditional Catholic teaching on just war. Elllacuría, far from being an enthusiast for the armed violence of the civil war in El Salvador, spent the last years of his life seeking a negotiated peace between the government and the revolutionary FMLN to enable a more just society to be built. When a highly unjust society suppresses all legal means for reform and uses violence to suppress dissent, armed revolution may become necessary to create a new political system for building a more just society.[16] This, of course, is exactly what English colonists in North America did in their own revolution, which they justified in their Declaration of Independence.

Ellacuría called the new humanity to which Christianity and authentic humanity must aspire a "civilization of poverty" (civilización de pobreza), what more traditionally is called "simple living." This civilization meets the basic necessities for all members, for food, housing, health, education, and work with dignity. The social predominates over the political, building communitarian relations that overcome excessive inequalities. Such societies are grounded neither in capitalist individualist consumerism nor Marxist collectivism, but in democratic socialism that builds solidarity and mutual help. These societies would be freed from all forms of international imperialism and dependency and control of their own resources. They would cultivate more contemplative and more communicative forms of popular culture. The new humanity would promote relations of love and solidarity with others, with special concern for those still left out or marginalized. While Ellacuría did not expect such societies to appear in perfected form in history, they should become the social ideal, the ideal toward which societies should aspire and seek to build by continual practical steps.[17] Far from being "obsolete," such hopes for an alternative society are ones that need to inspire us all the more in the twenty-first century.

IVONE GEBARA

Ivone Gebara is a Brazilian feminist theologian born in 1944 in São Paulo to immigrant parents from Syria and Lebanon. Her parents entertained the typical hopes of immigrant parents of good marriages for their three daughters. But Gebara was attracted to study and repelled by these social hopes of her parents. At the age of twenty-two, she graduated from the University of São Paulo in philosophy and joined the religious order of Notre Dame, Canoneses of St. Augustine. Gebara sought liberation from the demands of her family and a place to cultivate her desires for study and for work for social justice. She was, however, deeply affected by the strong opposition of her parents. Thus, early in her life, she experienced her own desires for liberation set in conflict with those she loved.[18]

In the 1970s Gebara studied philosophy and religion at Louvain University in Belgium, receiving a PhD. She taught for sixteen years in the Theological Institute in Recife, Brazil, which prepared pastoral leaders through immersion in the daily life of the poor. In the 1980s she read feminist theory and theology from Europe and North America and challenged the claims of her male colleagues that feminist thought was irrelevant for Latin Americans. She increasingly realized that feminism did not simply add an additional oppressed subject to liberation theology, but challenged the whole paradigm of classical Christian theology based on hierarchical dualisms of spirit over body and male over female. Her male colleagues, who had accepted her when she taught men's books and theology, became uncomfortable with her as she began to ask radically new questions.[19]

In 1990 when the new conservative bishop closed the seminary in Recife and fired its faculty, Gebara realized that her ability to work in such a setting had come to an end. She moved to a slum neighborhood in Camaragible in northern Brazil and worked with poor women and children. At the same time, she also began to lecture and teach short courses in the United States, Canada, and Europe. In 1994 she fell into a conflict with the Vatican and its Brazilian hierarchy because she was interviewed in the popular magazine *VEJA* and expressed her support for legalized abortion, based on her experiences with poor women. While not directly approving abortion, she suggested that it could be a lesser of evils in many cases. After Gebara had numerous meetings with the president of the Brazilian conference of bishops, he declared the case closed, but the Vatican kept after her.

On June 3, 1995, Gebara was instructed to refrain from speaking, teaching, and writing for two years and to go to Europe for "reeducation" in Catholic teaching. She returned to the University of Louvain, where she did a second PhD in theology and began a book on the nature of evil from a woman's perspective.[20] With her return to Brazil in 1997 Gebara continued to work closely with the ecofeminist network based in Chile, Con-spirando, and helped to organize several theological workshops on ecofeminist thought in Santiago, Chile, Recife, Brazil, and Washington, DC.

In that 1993 interview, Gebara traced the development of Latin American feminist theology over twenty years.[21] In the first stage, stimulated by the secular women's movement in Latin America and the translation of feminist theology from Europe and the United States, feminist theologians began to recognize that "we are oppressed as historical subjects. We discovered our oppression in the Bible, in theology, in our churches." The feminist challenge launched searches for female role models in the Bible: prophetesses and matriarchs, and female disciples of Jesus, such as Mary Magdalene.

The second stage of feminist theology turned to the "feminization of theological concepts. We began to discover the submerged feminine expressions for God in the Bible. We discovered God's maternal face in texts, such as Isaiah 49." During this period, women's roles expanded as teachers, catechists, and leaders of base Christian communities. Male liberation theologians began to include a few women in their conferences and publications to give the "women's perspective." Gebara calls these two stages "patriarchal feminism." It did not challenge Christian paradigms of humanity, the cosmos, and God, but simply added women to them.

Women were regarded as having distinct—sometimes even superior—moral insights and ways of being, compared to men, so it was good to add the "feminine dimension" to theology and pastoral life.

Gebara sees herself and others as pioneering a third, more radical feminist stage. She sees all theologies, including feminist theologies, as arising from distinct contexts and needing to own these contexts, speaking both within and yet not limited to their particularities. Gebara sees herself, not simply as adding the women's perspective to theology, but as dismantling the foundational patriarchal paradigm that has shaped the relationships of humans to each other, to nature, and to God. Hierarchical dualisms shaping cosmology, epistemology, and ethics must be overcome. Gebara starts from the plurality of human experiences, especially women's experiences, rather than a fixed set of hierarchical dualisms that divide God and creation as spirit over matter, male over female. She wishes to dismantle the false universalities of white male Western elites and to explore what might connect us all, as humans who are earth creatures and members of one cosmos.

Gebara speaks of herself as a privileged Brazilian woman—white, educated, and middle class—who has chosen to identify with the poorest Brazilians of the Northeast, mostly mixtures of black, white, and indigenous. The Northeast of Brazil is a region of violent contrasts of wealth and poverty shaped by centuries of colonialism, feudalism, and capitalism. A few have great power, while the majority are powerless; a few hold vast lands and wealth, while the many are landless and poor. Gebara's commitment to the oppressed reflects liberation theology's preferential option for the poor, but without the utopian confidence of the 1980s. Today the sheer pervasiveness of systemic and particular evils is overwhelming. By contrast, goodness often seems occasional and fragile. Moved by these daily experiences of evil, Gebara even speaks of the "immanence and transcendence of evil" and wonders if this is what the theologians traditionally called "original sin."[22]

Gebara speaks of doing theology in the midst of "noise and garbage," quite the opposite of the realm of monastic or ivory tower solitude and quiet that has been the traditional place for Christians to cultivate spirituality and theological reflection. The noise of her neighborhood is both the noise pollution of a dysfunctional modern industrialism, such as cars and trucks without mufflers, and the noisy responses of the poor who dwell in this area, the loud radios and quarrelling voices of those living in crowded conditions. The garbage is the waste discarded by the poor who lack proper sanitation. To live one's spirituality and to do one's theology amid noise and garbage is to do them in the context of oppression and violence, but also inspired by the vitality of the poor who manage to survive and even to celebrate in this context and despite it.[23]

Women theologians, Gebara notes, are coming to voice at time when women are becoming aware of being historical agents. It is a time when systems of domination built over millennia, both in the church and in society with religious and philosophical justifications, are coming apart and revealing themselves as unjust and destructive. Women theologians see through the successive layers of distortion that justify this oppressive system and reflect critically on our inherited symbols with our real questions from everyday experiences. Christian women must overcome the timidity and feelings of guilt to which patriarchal culture has socialized us. We must dare to approach these venerable theological constructs, with their claims to infallible authority, and to rethink them from the context of *lo cotidiano*, daily life.[24]

Gebara believes we should question the great theological dogmas, using women's daily experience, and she offers radical reinterpretations of such dogmas. She asks, "what human experiences do these dogmas actually represent and encode?" In one way, Gebara seems to see theology as a human construct, a projection on the heavens of our human relations and hopes. However, she understands that these relations go beyond the human; they include our relations with nature, with plants and animals, air, water, and earth, and with the cosmos as a context for all relations. The human experience of all these relations is the basis for doing theology. There is no God "out there" revealing "His nature" and "His plan" to us. We ourselves are the thinking part of the universe, we who imagine and create systems of interpretation. There is a reality out there larger than ourselves; God is that reality, which sustains all of life and is the source of our ever-renewed hopes in the midst of disappointment. This reality permeates life; God is not a spiritual "ego" outside of reality and over against the body. It is always we humans who are interpreting this reality we call God, who sustains our life and hope.[25]

The Trinity has been a particular focus in Gebara's deconstructing and reconstructing of Christian symbols.[26] She does not see the Trinity as a distant deity with three persons living outside the cosmos and controlling it remotely from above. Rather, the Trinity is a symbolic expression of the dynamic of life itself as a process of vital interrelational creativity. Life as interrelational creativity exists on every level of reality. As cosmos, it reveals itself in the whole process of cosmic unfolding and the interrelating of planets and galaxies. As earth, it shows itself as the dynamic interrelational process of life unfolding in the biosphere.[27] Each species embodies many differences, including human beings with their many races and cultures. Each person exists in a dynamic of creativity, plurality, and interdependency, of diversity and communion. We need to celebrate all of this diversity of human plurality of race and culture, affirming their mutuality with each other in one human earth community, and overcome the urge to set up one kind of difference as the universal and best and to make all the others inferior. The dynamic of life in vital interrelationship and diversity is the meaning of God as Trinity.

Gebara also raises the question of evil in relation to this understanding of the goodness of life as Trinity. What are the roots of evil and how is it reproduced? Her answer is that the nature of the life process is intrinsically limited and fragile. Life is reproduced in a process of both pain and joy, of birth and death and new birth.[28] Evil as tragedy is a natural part of life and inseparable from it. But humans also experience finitude, diversity, and death as threatening. In their quest for survival, humans have the urge to try to secure life permanently against death and to secure power as control to ward off vulnerability, and difference by subjugating the "other." Women, other races, other cultures, and the earth itself have been made into victims of this urge to control and secure life by one group, who then seek to secure power against difference, vulnerability, and death. Women have been particularly victimized because, as birth-givers, they are imagined to represent the vulnerability of the life process in its threatening power and difference from men.[29]

Out of this urge to control and secure life and power, elite men have arisen to shape systems of domination by which they attempt to secure a monopoly of power over life for themselves. In this way the dynamic of interrelation of differences is distorted into extreme imbalances of power and powerlessness, domination and violation, wealth and poverty.[30] Gebara notes that Christianity, among many religions, has aided such systems. The idea of a powerful invulnerable patriarchal God reflects this desire of elite men to control life immortally and to escape death. The powerless, on the other hand, create countermyths of great saviors who will defeat the oppressors by righteous violence and bring about a permanent state of bliss without death. Such messianic countermyths, including the utopias promoted by some spokesmen of liberation theology, tend to reproduce the system of violence.

We live at a time when this system of distortion has reached a crisis point, threatening to destroy planetary life itself. Such distorted relationships of power and subjugation are the meaning of evil in the sense of sin; i.e., unnatural and destructive evil, which humans have constructed but cannot and should not accept as necessary and inevitable. Humans need to struggle to overcome this destructive evil, for the sake of both interhuman justice and the defense of life.

For Gebara, religion plays an ambiguous role in this construction of a system of evil, in the sense of sin. Most religions have justified this urge to control and dominate by the powerful. Jesus, Gebara believes, was a different kind of prophetic figure who sought to break through the reproduction of the cycle of violence. While taking the side of the victims, he also called the privileged to join with the poor in a community of mutual service and celebration. The dominant system of both political power and religious privilege rejected his message and killed him. His followers betrayed him by turning his vision of shared community into a new warrior savior myth upon whom a new system of imperial power could be built.[31]

Gebara proposes that feminist theologians should reject absolutes of all kinds. They should not imagine either a paradise of the beginning when there was no death or vulnerability, nor a paradise of the future when there will be no more death or vulnerability. We all need to withdraw from these projections and come to terms with the fragile and ambiguous nature of life always mixed with pain and death. Rather than seeking to flee to a future Reign of God freed from all evil, we need to learn to share with each other our fragile good and vulnerable joys and sorrows in a way that is truly mutual. We need to do what we can in our limited ways to dismantle the great systems of domination and exploitation, but not with the illusion that all pain and finitude will thereby disappear. Rather, to lessen unjust imbalances of power is at the same time to accept those limits of life that are always fraught with tragedy, as well as with joy and renewed hope.[32]

We must, as Gebara puts it, "take the side of the serpent" of Genesis 3, refusing the orders of the patriarchal God that keep us in a state of childish dependency. We can then recognize that the fragile fruit of the tree of life is indeed lovely and good for discernment. We can eat this fruit with relish, making it a part of our bodies and hearts. This is the real and possible redemption of life on earth. But it is real and possible only when we put aside the impossible redemptions of final conquest of all limits in a realm of immortal life untouched by sorrow, vulnerability, and finitude.

Gebara's theology, written from the 1990s into the early twenty-first century, appears quite different in style and tone from that of Ignacio Ellacuría, written in the midst of the daily threats of state violence in the civil war of El Salvador in the 1980s. This difference is partly due to new situations in Latin America where poverty and violence are no less threatening, but are experienced as more global and faceless. It is partly due to new dimensions offered through women's perspectives and from the ecological crisis. Yet for all their differences, they share many similarities. Gebara neither refutes nor supercedes Ellacuría, and Ellacuría's work does not stand in judgment on Gebara. Both voices must be probed deeply and respectfully in the ongoing quest for a life-giving theology and for just communities.

EPILOGUE

Can Men Be Ordained?

A synod of bishops from the four corners of the earth and a panoply of Mother Superiors recently converged on the Holy City of Rome to consider the vexed question of the ordination of men. The Holy See has received many tearful appeals from the cruder sex claiming to have a call to the priesthood directly from God herself.

Her Holiness has firmly replied to these appeals that the call must have been a wrong number. Our Holy Mother in Heaven would never call to the sacred ministry those so obviously disqualified by reason of gender. However, the men refused to take no for an answer. Throwing down their picks and shovels, they declared that they would do no more maintenance work for the church until there was equality of rites.

The men sent petitions to the Holy See filled with arguments for the ordination of men, both theological and practical. Although, of course, they could cite no example of Jesus himself, the incarnation of Holy Wisdom, since he had evidently ordained no men to the priesthood (or women either).

Finally, Her Holiness decided to gather the Holy Mothers of the church together, with a number of the best qualified *peritae* (women theological and scriptural experts), who had spent a lifetime studying the odd characteristics of the male gender—from a safe distance, of course. They hoped to come up with a definitive answer, once and for all, to the question of whether men can be ordained.

After long and careful study, in which the Holy Mothers had enjoyed many a good laugh on the subject of men and their foibles, the Holy Mothers drew up a final decree defining the reasons why men cannot be ordained. The decree was proclaimed by Her Holiness *ad urbi et orbi* (to the city of Rome and to the whole world), and the Holy Mothers departed for their respective seats of Wisdom, feeling very pleased with themselves. The decree *ad hominem* stated the weighty reasons for their gut prejudices to their satisfaction and, it was hoped, for all time.

The first part of the decree deduced a good many reasons from men's biological and psychological natures that disqualified them from the priesthood. It was said, first of all, that men were too violent and emotional to be priests. Anyone who has watched groups of men at football games, ice hockey, or soccer matches, not to mention political conventions, has seen their volatile tendencies and penchant for solving conflicts with fisticuffs. To ordain such creatures would be to risk disgraceful brawls at the altar. The male proneness to violence surely disqualifies them from representing the One who incarnates graciousness and peace.

The cruder and heavier physical frame of the male clearly marks him for the physical tasks of society: digging ditches, mending roofs, carrying heavy loads, and the like. The finer, more spiritual roles in society are intended by our

Mother in Heaven for those of more delicate, refined spirits and bodies: women.

It was also felt that men were needed for military defense. "A man's place is in the army," declared one of the *peritae*, and all the Holy Mothers nodded in agreement. Besides, men would look silly in long dresses, lace over blouses, large plush hats, and red satin slippers. The sacred garb is clearly intended for women.

Profound matters of a theological nature were also discussed. One *perita* had prepared a long paper proving from the symbolic order that men could not be ordained. The division of humanity into female and male is a profound mystery that symbolizes the relationship of the transcendent and the immanent, the spiritual and the material, heaven and earth. Women represent the spiritual realm, men the material. The material must be ruled over by the spiritual, just as Holy Wisdom presides from the Heavens over the physical cosmos as her household.

Moreover since the church is female in her essence, those who represent her should be female as well. There should be a physical resemblance between the priest and the church as Holy Mother. Obviously this means that all priests should be mature women. The church is also said to be Bride of Christ and brides are female. The priest, as the representative of the church in relation to Christ, represents Christ's bride. Therefore only women can be priests.

Finally it was noted that most of the people who come to church are women. Men tend to stand outside the doors of the church, gossiping, or sneak off to sports matches. To have a man on the altar might distract women from their prayers. It was solemnly observed that men are actually sexually attractive to some women. For women to have to sit listening to men preach and watching them stomping around the sanctuary might cause their thoughts to descend from the higher to the lower realms.

It was hoped that with so many clear reasons, from the theological as well as the practical spheres, against the ordination of men, the matter would be settled once and for all. Male impertinence would be silenced, and they would sink back into their proper sphere, namely, hard physical labor. *Roma Locuta: Causa Finita* (Rome has spoken, the matter is finished).

Acknowledgments

A longer version of the material in the introduction to this book was given as a talk at the summer school of Boston College in July 2006.

Parts of the material in chapter 4 on women-church appeared in the article "The Women-church Movement in Contemporary Christianity" in *Women's Leadership in Marginal Religions: Explorations Outside the Mainstream*, ed. Catherine Wessinger, pages 196–210, copyright, 1993 by the Board of Trustees of the University of Illinois. Used by permission of the University of Illinois Press. Parts of the material in chapter 5 on the discipleship of equals appeared in the chapter on "The Ecclesiology of Women-church: Ministry and Community," in Rosemary Ruether, *Women-Church: Theology and Practice* (San Francisco, CA: Harper and Row, 1986), pages 75–95. Chapter 6 on Latin America liberation theology will appear in a longer version in Miguel A. de la Torre, *The Hope of Liberation in World Religions* (Waco, TX: Baylor University Press, 2008), used by permission of Baylor University Press. The material in the epilogue appeared originally in the *National Catholic Reporter*, under the title "Uppity Men Aim at the Altar," May 13, 1988, page 15.

Notes

2: REPRODUCTIVE RIGHTS AND
THE VATICAN'S "PRO-LIFE ETHICS"

1. See Robert McClory, *Turning Point: The Inside Story of the Papal Birth Control Commission* (New York: Crossroad, 1995), 38–41.

2. *Contraception and Holiness*, edited by Gregory Baum, a Canadian Augustinian theologian; *Contraception and Catholics*, by Louis Dupre of Georgetown University; *What Modern Catholics Think About Birth Control*, a collection of essays edited by William Birmingham, editor of the lay journal *Cross Currents*; and a collection of personal testimonies edited by lay theologian Michael Novak, *The Experience of Marriage*.

3. McClory, 114, 127–29.

4. Ibid., 110–11, 129–32.

5. Ibid., 122.

6. Ibid., 140–46. See also Philip Kaufman, *Why You Can Disagree and Remain a Faithful Catholic* (New York: Crossroads, 1991).

7. McClory, 149–50.

8. McClory, 148. See also *Andrew Greeley, American Catholics Since the Council: An Unauthorized Report* (Chicago: Thomas More, 1985).

9. This is the argument of Robert Blair Kaiser's book on the birth control commission, *The Politics of Sex and Religion* (Kansas City, MO: Leaven Press, 1985).

10. See "Family Planning Under Attack" on the Web site for Catholics for Contraception.

11. See www.seechange.org.

12. This information on the Bush administration and reproductive rights comes from J. Bernstein, "The Bush Administration's Assault on Women, a Chronology," *NARAL*, February 24, 2003.

13. "To Make a Seamless Garment, Use a Single Piece of Cloth," in Patricia Beattie and Thomas Shannon, eds., *Abortion and Catholicism: The American Debate* (New York: Crossroads, 1988), 279–96.

14. See Dan Dombrowski and Robert Delite, *A Brief Liberal Catholic Defense of Abortion* (Champaign-Urbana, IL: University of Illinois Press, 2000).

15. See Jamie Doward, "Pope 'Obstructed' Sex Abuse Inquiry," *The Observer*, April 24, 2005; see http://observer.guardian .co.uk/international/story/0,6903,1469055,00.html.ying.

4: WOMEN-CHURCH

1. Some Christian groups in America, such as the Congregationalists, Unitarians, Universalists, and Methodists, had already begun to ordain women in the nineteenth century. After World War II, the Lutheran and Reformed Churches in Europe, and the United Methodist Church and the Presbyterian Church in the United States, among other Protestants, began ordaining women. By 1974 the main struggles over this issue in American Protestant churches were in the Episcopal church and in the more fundamentalist churches, such as the Southern Baptists.

2. Rosemary Ruether, "Spirituality and Justice: Popular Church Movements in the United States," in *A Democratic Catholic Church: The Reconstruction of Roman Catholicism*, ed. Rosemary Radford Ruether and Eugene C. Bianchi (New York: Crossroad, 1992), 189–93.

3. Janet Kalven, "Women Breaking Boundaries: The Grail and Feminism," *Journal of Feminist Studies in Religion*, no. 1 (spring 1989): 119–42.

4. Mary C. Seegers, "The Loyal Opposition: Catholics for a

Free Choice," in *The Catholic Church and the Politics of Abortion: A View from the States*, ed. Timothy A. Byrnes and Mary C. Seegers (Boulder, CO: Westview Press, 1992), 169–87.

5. Norene Carter, "Entering the Sanctuary: The Episcopalian Story," in *Women of Spirit: Female Leadership in the Jewish and Christian Traditions*, ed. Rosemary R. Ruether and Eleanor McLaughlin (New York: Simon and Schuster, 1979), 356–72.

6. Anne Marie Gardiner, ed., *Women and Catholic Priesthood: An Expanded Vision: Proceedings of the Detroit Ordination Conference* (New York: Paulist, 1976).

7. See *Women Priests: A Catholic Commentary on the Vatican Declaration*, ed. Leonard Swidler and Arlene Swidler (New York: Paulist Press, 1977).

8. See www.romancatholicwomenpriests.org.

9. The women's groups were LCWR (the Leadership Conference of Women Religious), NCAN (the National Coalition of American Nuns), NAWR (the National Assembly of Women Religious), WOC (the Women's Ordination Conference), St. Joan's Alliance, the Institute for Women Today, Christian Feminists, Las Hermanas, the National Black Sisters Conference, the National Sisters Vocation Conference, and Priests for Equality. Donna Quinn, founder of Chicago Catholic Women, provided me with the information on this history.

10. In April 1996 I sent out a questionnaire to the list of thirty-one members of the Women-Church Convergence. I received a response from eighteen of these groups. This response was from a member of the Feminist Interest Group of the School Sisters of St. Francis.

6: LIBERATION FOR THE POOR AND OPPRESSED

1. Eduardo Galeano, *The Open Veins of Latin America: Five Centuries of the Pillage of a Continent* (New York: Monthly Review Press, 1973).

2. *Teología de Liberación: Perspectivas* (Lima, Peru: CEP, 1971).

3. The most denunciatory Vatican document was *Libertatis Nuntius*, 1984. Vatican documents in 1986 are more conciliatory. See Alfred T. Hennelly, *Liberation Theology: A Documentary History* (New York: Orbis Books, 1990). Juan Luis Segundo responded with a book-length critique of the 1984 Vatican encyclical: see his *Theology and the Church: A Response to Cardinal Ratzinger and a Warning to the Whole Church*, trans. John W. Dierckmeier (Minneapolis, MN: Winston Press, 1985).

4. See Harvey Cox, *The Silencing of Leonardo Boff* (Oak Park, IL: Meyer-Stone, 1988).

5. Among Protestants that early contributed to liberation theology are Ruben Alves, whose *Theology of Human Hope*, appeared in 1969; Julio de Santa Ana; and José Miguez Bonino.

6. See the critique of these claims of the "death" of liberation theology by the radical orthodoxy movement by Finnish student of liberation theology Elina Vuola, "Radical Eurocentrism: The Crisis and Death of Latin American Liberation Theology and Recipes for Its Improvement," in Rosemary R. Ruether and Marion Grau, eds., *Interpreting the Postmodern: Responses to Radical Orthodoxy* (New York: T&T Clark, 2006), 57–75.

7. For Ellacuría's Zibirian philosophy of liberation, see David I. Gandolfo, "Ignacio Ellacuría," *The Internet Encyclopedia of Philosophy*, www.iep.edu/e/ellacuria.

8. Ignacio Ellacuría, "Historia de la Salvación," *Escritos Teológicos*, vol. 1 (San Salvador: UCA, 2001), 597–601.

9. Ellacuriá, "Dimensión politico del messanism de Jesús," *Escritos Teológicos*, vol. 2, 33–66.

10. Ellacuría, "Los Pobres, Lugar Teológico en América Latina," *Escritos Teológicos*, vol. 1, 141–42.

11. Ellacuría, "El pueblo crucificado," *Escritos Teológicos*, vol. 2, 137–70. The English translation of this essay is found in *Mysterium Liberationis: Fundamental Concepts of Liberation Theology*, ed. Ignacio Ellacuría and Jon Sobrino (Maryknoll, NY: Orbis Books, 1993), 580–603.

12. Ellacuría, "La Iglesia de los Pobres; sacramento histórico de liberación," *Escritos Teológicos*, vol. 1, 445.

13. Ellacuría, "Annuncio del Reino y credibilidad de la Iglesia," *Escritos Teológicos*, vol. 1, 659–98.

14. For a good account of Ellacuría's life and thought and the effects of his death on forcing an end to the civil war, see Teresa Whitfield, *Paying the Price: Ignacio Ellacuría and the Murdered Jesuits of El Salvador* (Philadelphia, PA: Temple University Press, 1994).

15. See Teresa Whitfield, *Paying the Price*, 221–22. On April 15, 1990, Mirian Davidson wrote in her review of Paul Sigmund's *Liberation Theology at the Crossroads* that "Fr. Ellacuría was one of several Central American theologians who advocated revolutionary counter-violence to the poor and oppressed of El Salvador" (Whitfield, 454, note 67).

16. See Ellacuría, "Violencia y Cruz," *Escritos Teológicos*, vol. 2, 454–81.

17. Ellacuría, "Utopia y profetismo desde América Latina," *Escritos Teológicos*, vol. 2, 264–89. English translation in *Mysterium Liberationis,* 289–328.

18. See Gebara's recent autobiography, *Las Aguas de mi Pozo: Reflexiones sobre Experiencias de Libertad* (Montevideo, Uruguay: Double Clic, 2005), 41–70.

19. See her remarks on her experiences with responses to feminism by her colleagues in Las Aguas de mi Pozo, 133–64; also in *El Rostro Oculto del Mal: Una Teología desde la experiencia de las Mujeres* (Madrid: Editorial Trotta, 2000), 78–81.

20. The book was originally written in French as *Le mal au feminin* (1999) and was published in English as *Out of the Depths: Women's Experience of Evil and Salvation* (Minneapolis: Fortress Press, 2002) and in Spanish as *El Rostro Oculto del Mal: Una Teología desde la experiencia de las Mujeres.*

21. "Ecofeminism and Panentheism," interviewed by Mary Judy Ress, *Creation Spirituality* (November/December 1993), 9–11.

22. *El Rostro Oculto del Mal*, 81–86.

23. Ivone Gebara, "A Cry for Life from Latin America," in *Spirituality of the Third World: A Cry for Life*, ed. K.C. Abraham

and Bernadette Mbuy-Beya (Maryknoll, NY: Orbis Press, 1994), 109–18.

24. Speaking from daily life or *lo cotidiano*, is a typical theme in Gebara and in Latin American feminism generally; see her *Intuiciones ecofeministas: Ensayo para repensar el conocimiento y la religion* (Madrid: Editorial Trotta, 2000), 38–42; also *El Rostro Oculto del Mal*, 106–7.

25. For Gebara's views on God, see *Longing for Running Water: Ecofeminism and Liberation* (Minneapolis: Fortress, 1999), 101–35: also *Intuiciones Ecofeministas*, 133–49; and *El Rostro Oculto del Mal*, 185–220.

26. See Gebara, *Longing for Running Water*, 137–71; also in *Teología a Ritmo de Mujer* (Madrid: San Pablo, 1995), 109–56. A long version of this essay on the Trinity was published in Portuguese as *Trinidade; palavra sobre coisas velhas e novas, una perspectiva ecofeminista* (São Paulo: Paulinas, 1994).

27. Gebara is much influenced by and follows the perspective of Brian Swimme and Thomas Berry's *New Universe Story* (San Francisco: HarperSanFrancisco, 1994).

28. See her "En los Origenes del Mal," and "Cuerpo de Mujer," in *Teología a Ritmo de Mujer*, 39–52 and 71–88.

29. Gebara explores this theme in "Las causas profundas del prejuicio en relación con la mujer" in the essay "Las incómodas hijas de Eva," in *Levánte y Anda: Algunos Aspectos del caminar de la mujer en América Latina* (México, D.F.: Editiones Dabar, 1995), 52–59.

30. *Teología a Ritmo de Mujer*, 146–56.

31. See her chapter on "cristología fundamental," in *Teología a Ritmo de Mujer*, 53–70.

32. This view of fragile and partial goods shared in the midst of ambiguous life is found throughout Gebara's writing. See her chapter on "la experiencia de salvación de las mujeres," in *El Rostro Oculo de Mal*, 145–83.